THE STOUR VALLEY RAILWAY

B.D.J. V

EARM PUBLICATIONS

a division of East Anglian Railway Museum (Trading) Ltd.

EARM PUBLICATIONS

Chappel & Wakes Colne Station, Colchester, CO6 2DS. Tel. 01206 242524
a division of East Anglian Railway Museum (Trading) Ltd., the trading subsidiary
of East Anglian Railway Museum, a Registered Charity No. 1001579

Publishing History:
First published by Stour Valley Railway Preservation Society
Revised and updated edition published by East Anglian Railway Museum 1987
Further revised, updated and expanded edition published by EARM Publications
2008

ISBN 0 95553121 1 6
978 0 9553121 1 3
British Library Cataloguing In Publication Data.
A catalogue record for this book is available from the British Library
© East Anglian Railway Museum 2008
Typeset and designed by EARM Publications

Printed by Crescent Card Company, Tiptree, Colchester, Essex

*This book is dedicated to all those whose interest, enthusiasm and hard work has
served to keep this beautiful line alive and remembered*

Acknowledgments

This is the third edition of B.D.J. Walsh's book on the Stour Valley Railway, a
line which he knew well from his earliest days. Sadly, just before he was due to
start updating work he passed away, and as a result the work has been completed
by a number of volunteers from the East Anglian Railway Museum, in which Mr
Walsh was an active member of from its foundation. Thanks go to all the following
people for their assistance with the updating: Alan Sermons, Michael Stanbury,
Mark House, Mark Cornell and John Mann.

The Museum would like to express its appreciation for help with this book to
members of The Great Eastern Railway Society which exists to record and celebrate
that company and all its works and successors. The East Anglian Railway Museum
was founded in 1968 as the Stour Valley Railway Preservation Society, taking its
new name in 1986. It is a Registered Charity and Registered Museum seeking to
preserve and demonstrate the history of railways of the Eastern Counties. Full
details may be found on the Museum web-site at www.earm.co.uk.

The Coming of the Railway

Sudbury, a busy and prosperous market town - famous as the birthplace of Gainsborough, and as the "Eatanswill" of Dickens' "Pickwick Papers" - is situated on the south west border of Suffolk and on the northern bank of the River Stour which for a considerable distance marks the boundary between Essex and Suffolk. The town, which had a population of about 5,000 in the 1840's, lies within a fertile and productive agricultural area, and was a centre of much trade even before the coming of the railway, while the River Stour, although navigable only with some difficulty, had served as a means of communication since the undertakers of the River Stour Navigation had completed their works in about 1713.

The completion of the Eastern Counties Railway to Colchester, in 1843, left Sudbury some 11 miles to the north, and it was to facilitate trade between Colchester and the Sudbury area that the Colchester, Stour Valley, Sudbury and Halstead Railway was projected. The company was incorporated by the Act 9 & 10 (Vic. cap. lxxvi of 26th June, 1846) with a capital of £250,000, and was authorised to construct a line from the E.C.R. station at Marks Tey, five miles south-west of Colchester, to Sudbury, with intermediate stations at Chappel and Bures - a total distance of 11 miles 53 chains. A triangular junction at Marks Tey was originally envisaged, but in fact the spur joining the main line on the London side of Marks Tey station was never built, and the actual junction has always faced Colchester. The company was also authorised to construct a branch from Chappel to Halstead, as well as a line running from the Eastern Union Railway at Colchester to the riverside port of Colchester, known as the Hythe.

By the Act 10 & 11 (Vic. Cap. xi of 8th June, 1847) the company obtained powers to build an extension line from Sudbury via Long Melford to Clare, with a branch from Long Melford to Lavenham. Two other Acts were obtained by the company on the same day. One of these - 10 & 11 (Vic. Cap. xviii) - empowered the company to build yet a further extension from Lavenham to Bury St. Edmunds, while the other - 10 & 11 (Vic. Cap. xxi) - authorised the company to lease the whole of its undertaking to the Ipswich and Bury St. Edmunds Railway, which itself, however, had already entered into a working arrangement with the Eastern Union Railway, and which was absorbed by the last-named company under powers contained in the Act 10 & 11 (Vic. cap. clxxiv) dated 9th July, 1847.

In the meantime, the short 1 3/4 mile branch from Colchester to Hythe had been constructed, and was opened for the reception of freight traffic on 31st March, 1847. The first train ran on the following day. The line remained in use for freight traffic only until the extension from Hythe to Wivenhoe had been built by the Tendring Hundred Railway, and the whole line from Colchester to Wivenhoe was opened for passenger traffic on 8th May, 1863. This line became part of the route from Colchester to Walton-on-Naze and Clacton-on-Sea, but of course does not figure further in our story.

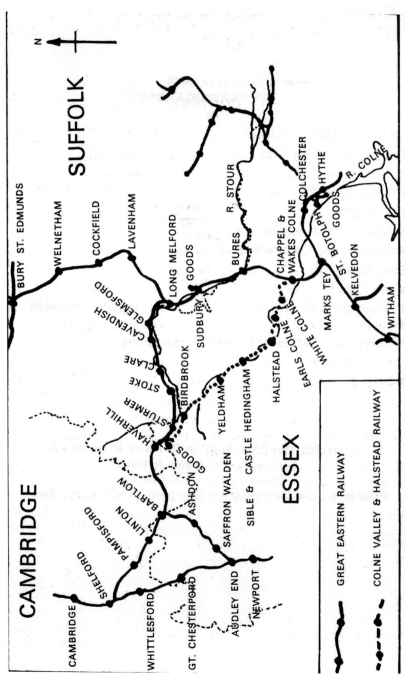

Stour Valley Railway and adjoining Lines showing pre-grouping ownership

CAMBRIDGE

SUFFOLK

ESSEX

N

BURY ST. EDMUNDS
WELNETHAM
COCKFIELD
LAVENHAM
LONG MELFORD
GOODS
BURES
R. STOUR
GLEMSFORD
CAVENDISH
SUDBURY
CLARE
STOKE
BIRDBROOK
STURMER
HAVERHILL
YELDHAM
GOODS
ASHDON
BARTLOW
LINTON
PAMPISFORD
SHELFORD
CAMBRIDGE
WHITTLESFORD
GT. CHESTERFORD
AUDLEY END
NEWPORT
SAFFRON WALDEN
SIBLE & CASTLE HEDINGHAM
HALSTEAD
EARLS COLNE
WHITE COLNE
CHAPPEL &
WAKES COLNE
MARKS TEY
ST. BOTOLPHS
COLCHESTER
HYTHE
GOODS
R. COLNE
KELVEDON
WITHAM

GREAT EASTERN RAILWAY

COLNE VALLEY & HALSTEAD RAILWAY

4

The Eastern Union Railway worked the Hythe branch from the beginning, and by an agreement dated 17th November, 1848, the whole of the undertaking of the Colchester, Stour Valley, Sudbury & Halstead Railway was leased to the Eastern Union Railway for 999 years at a rate calculated on the basis of 6% of the former company's expenditure on the line.

The line from Marks Tey to Sudbury was single track, but was built by Jackson, the contractor, to accommodate a second track if the traffic developed sufficiently to warrant it. Crossing loops were provided at Chappel (3 miles 38 chains from Marks Tey) and at Bures (6 miles 64 chains), although in the early years of the line a shuttle service sufficed for the traffic offering. The line was opened throughout from Marks Tey to Sudbury for all traffic on 2nd July, 1849, with little ceremony, and the passengers arriving at Sudbury by the directors' special train were left to wander about the town until lunch was ready. The triumphal arch which had been erected at Marks Tey was dislodged by the locomotive, which carried the laurels and other decorations festooned around its chimney and dome throughout the journey to Sudbury! The principal engineering feature of the line was - and still is - the Chappel Viaduct, by which the railway is carried over the valley of the River Colne. This imposing structure is 1,066 feet in length, has 32 arches each of 30 ft. span, and its maximum height is 75 ft. It was built at a cost of £32,000 and some 7,000,000 bricks were used in its construction.

The original train service consisted of four trains in each direction on weekdays only, and the fares charged were those authorised by the Act of 1846, namely 3d per mile first class, 2d per mile second class and 1d per mile third class. Only one train

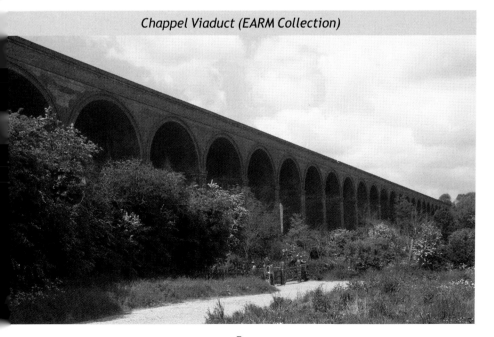

Chappel Viaduct (EARM Collection)

in each direction conveyed third class passengers. By the end of 1850, one train in each direction ran through to and from Colchester, and an additional train ran between Marks Tey and Sudbury. In 1852, two Sunday trains in each direction were introduced, both conveying passengers of all three classes.

By the Eastern Union Railway Arrangements Act, 1852 (15 & 16 Vic. cap. cxlviii), it was provided that, as from 1st July, 1852, the sum of £9,500 per annum should be paid to the Colchester, Stour Valley, Sudbury & Halstead Railway for the rent of their line instead of the fluctuating amount previously agreed.

On 1st January, 1854, the Eastern Counties Railway leased the Eastern Union Railway's lines and took over their working under an agreement made on 19th December, 1853, which was retrospectively sanctioned by an Act (17 & 18 Vic. cap. ccxx) dated 7th August, 1854. Consequently, the Eastern Counties Railway also assumed responsibility for the working of the Colchester, Stour Valley, Sudbury & Halstead Railway.

As the powers of the last-named company to build a branch to Halstead had now expired, a new company - the Colne Valley & Halstead Railway - was promoted by local interests, and was incorporated by an Act of 30th June, 1856 (19 & 20 Vic Cap. lxi) to construct a line to Halstead from a junction with the Stour Valley line at Chappel. After difficult and protracted negotiations with the Eastern Counties Railway, it was agreed that the Colne Valley company should be entitled to construct their junction at Chappel for a payment of £1,500 to the ECR, and the line to Halstead was formally opened on 16th April, 1860. A further Act of 13th August 1859 (22 & 23 Vic. cap. cxxii) had been obtained, authorising the Colne Valley company to extend its line from Halstead to Haverhill, and the first section, as far as Hedingham was opened to all traffic on 1st July, 1861. The next section, to Yeldham, was opened on 26th May, 1862 and Haverhill was reached on 10th May, 1863.

In the meantime, the Eastern Counties Railway continued to work the Stour Valley line, maintaining the strained relations which usually subsisted between the ECR and the small companies whose lines it worked. Early in 1857, for instance when Horatio Love had been appointed the new Chairman of the Eastern Counties Railway, growing dissatisfaction on the Stour Valley line was expressed by a memorial presented to him by the inhabitants of Sudbury and its neighbourhood, complaining of high fares, slow trains and unpunctuality. It was alleged that the last train to Sudbury at night was an hour late on average, and the memorialists commented: *"The reason seems to be that luggage trucks are invariably attached to this train at Marks Tey (doubtless in violation of the Act of Parliament), during which the passengers are confined in the carriages and are constantly shunted about for the space of 20 minutes before leaving."*

It was further stated that nobody from Sudbury could reach London, except on Mondays, until 12.55 p.m., although from the contemporary timetables this appears to be incorrect, at any rate in the case of first and second class passengers as there was a connection off the 7.15 a.m. Sudbury to Marks Tey train which reached Bishopsgate at 10.05 a.m. The memorial also complained of the price

charged for small parcels, the rates for which seemed:-
"to be altogether arbitrary, at the decision of the stationmaster,"... *"and of the almost universally bad and dirty state of the carriages"*,
and the junction at Marks Tey at which it was said:-
"The shed there, termed waiting room, is the only enclosure for first, second and third class passengers indiscriminately - a place alike unfitted for all classes, into which no person ventures excepting under the direst necessity of a stress of weather or other unfortunate circumstance. At this place it seems to be the practice unnecessarily to detain passengers for the arrival of trains."

No doubt these complaints were somewhat exaggerated as the trains were booked to run between Marks Tey and Sudbury in timings varying between 28 and 45 minutes, which was not unduly slow for a branch line in 1857, while the passenger fares conformed to the scale authorised by the Act of 1846. However, the complaints were perhaps the result largely of annoyance engendered by the slow level of speed of the ECR main line services at that time, which was worse than on most trunk routes.

As the Colne Valley & Halstead Railway remedied the omission of the Stour Valley company to build a line to Halstead, so another local concern attempted to make up for the Stour Valley Railway's failure to construct its projected lines to

Johnson 0-4-4T No.169 derailed between Lavenham and Long Melford whilst working the 4.5pm Bury to Marks Tey train on 17th October 1891. Two of the coaches turned on their sides, but there were no fatalities, and only eleven people were injured. (B.D.J. Walsh collection)

Clare and Bury St. Edmunds. In the event, it was obliged to abandon the idea of reaching Bury St. Edmunds, and it emerged as the Sudbury & Clare Railway , incorporated by the Act of 23rd July, 1860 (23 & 24 Vic. cap. clxiii) and was empowered to build a line from Sudbury to Clare via Melford. Scarcely had these powers been obtained, however, before the local company was absorbed by the Eastern Counties Railway, which at once sought extended powers for a line from Sudbury, via Melford, Clare and Haverhill to a junction with the London-Cambridge main line at Shelford, together with a branch from Melford to Bury St. Edmunds.

At the same time, the Colne Valley & Halstead Company, which had also received the minimum of co-operation from the Eastern Counties Railway, sought powers to extend its line to Cambridge in one direction and to Colchester in the other, in order to free itself permanently from the shackles of the ECR. Indeed, it was the Colne Valley's intention, in the event of it's Bill being successful, to lease the whole of it's line to the London & North Western Railway, which itself was soon to reach Cambridge from Bletchley via Bedford.

After a strongly contested struggle, however, the Colne Valley bill was rejected, and the Eastern Counties Railway obtained its Act (24 & 25 Vic. cap. ccxxxi) on 6th August 1861. Thus it was that LNWR "Jumbos" and "Precedents" never became destined to be seen at Colchester!

By this time, however, the Eastern Counties Railway had leased or taken over the working of all the major railways in East Anglia, and a scheme was prepared for the amalgamation of the Eastern Counties, Eastern Union, East Anglian, Newmarket and Norfolk Railways into a new undertaking to be known as the Great Eastern Railway. The Act sanctioning this amalgamation - the Great Eastern Railway Act, 1862 (25 & 26 Vic. cap. ccxxiii) obtained the Royal assent on 7th August, 1862, but took effective retrospectively from 1st July of that year. This Act also authorised anew the construction of sections of line from Sudbury to Melford, Melford to Clare, Clare to Shelford, and Melford to Bury St. Edmunds, as well as a connecting line at Haverhill between the Colne Valley & Halstead Railway and the Great Eastern Railway. The Engineers for the new lines were G P Bidder and Robert Sinclair; Thomas Brassey & Co were the contractors.

Construction of these lines began at the Shelford end. There were complaints locally that the works were not being carried out expeditiously, and the Bury Free Press reported on 19 March 1864:

"GREAT EASTERN RAILWAY COMPANY: The Parliamentary Committee have decided not to grant the application of this company an extension of time to complete the branches now in progress, consequently we may look for a little more expedition in the construction of the line between the town and Sudbury than has been manifested. The time fixed of its completion is the 1st of August next".

The section from Shelford to the G.E.R. station at Haverhill was opened to all traffic on 1st June, 1865.

The passenger service over the new line consisted of 3 trains per day in each direction on weekdays, and one on Sundays between Shelford and Haverhill (GE)

Sudbury goods yard, forming part of the original terminal station, in 1911. In the right background the passenger station on a sharp curve beyond the footbridge carrying a public footpath over the running lines. Lime works sidings are in the right foreground, with three Allen & Boggis lime wagons in the loop. Photograph from the Windwood Collection, courtesy of the National Railway Museum

third class passengers being conveyed by one of the weekday trains in each direction, as well as on the Sunday trains. On the Marks Tey-Sudbury section, there were now four trains down and five up on weekdays, including two in each direction on Sundays. Third class passengers were conveyed on two trains in each direction daily, including Sundays. The freight service included a through GER goods train which ran between Cambridge and Wivenhoe, via the Colne Valley Railway and Colchester. This train continued to run after the GER through route had been opened, and was not withdrawn until 1867. It was worked in each direction by two Stothert and Slaughter 0-6-0 locomotives with open cabs, numbered 1570 and 1580, which had been built in 1846 and were rebuilt with new boilers in 1866.

The Bury Free Press carried updated reports nearly every week as opening approached: on 3 June 1865 it reported "that traffic will be commenced upon it in July". Three weeks later they reported that all staff had been appointed and were in position. In the issue of 1 July 1865 it was advised that it was intended to open the line from Sudbury to Bury "on Monday next"; the following week's issue advised that the Government Inspector, Colonel Yolland, had inspected the line between

Bury and Sudbury the previous Tuesday and the next day the line from Long Melford to Haverhill: approval for opening was forthcoming.

However, before opening there was a serious accident at Melford. The Bury Free Press of 22 July 1865 reported that "on Saturday last" a train of empty trucks conveying workmen had run into a rake of wagons in a siding due to incorrect working of the points. Three men were killed in the collision, and a number of other serious injuries resulted.

The remainder of the new lines, from Haverhill to Sudbury and from Melford to Bury St. Edmunds, were opened on 9th August 1865. At Sudbury, the construction of the new line necessitated the diversion of the old line from Marks Tey in a westward direction, then curving around towards the north skirting the town of Sudbury on the west side. A new passenger station with two platforms was built on this curve. The Bury Free Press of 28 February 1864 announced that a new station would be built at Sudbury:

"In consequence of the extension of the railway to Melford, Cavendish, Clare and Bury, it has been decided to erect a new passenger station at Sudbury, about 200 yards from the present one, with new approaches in two directions from the town. The site will be at the back of the large goods shed. The station will be far more commodious than the old one and will be fitted with every convenience of a first class character. The new railway is expected to be completed and opened by the 1st July 1864".

However, the new station was still not completed in time for the opening over thirteen months later than planned, and the Bury Free Press of 19 August 1865 advised that there had been many complaints as "all that is erected is a common waiting shed for the issuing of tickets and two platforms. There is no shelter or room of any kind and the new station is only rising from the ground". The completion date of the new building appears to have gone unrecorded, but it is likely to have been towards the end of 1865. The old single-platform terminus became part of the goods yard, but was demolished in 1985/6 and a superstore was built on the site. The original small locomotive shed was demolished in 1952.

Within a few weeks of opening there was a serious accident at Welnetham, when the 6.23 train from Sudbury to Bury St Edmunds derailed and fell down a low embankment, with the locomotive becoming embedded in the ground. Fortunately there were neither any serious injuries nor fatalities.

The first Cheap Day excursion to London took place on Thursday 21 September 1865 at the following times and fares:

Bury	5.45	10/- (50p)	First Class
		5/- (25p)	Covered carriages
Welnetham	6.00	10/- (50p)	First Class
		5/- (25p)	Covered carriages
Lavenham	6.15	8/- (40p)	First Class
		4/- (20p)	Covered carriages

Melford   6.30 7/- (35p) First Class
                 3/6 (17^1/2p) Covered carriages

The train was scheduled to arrive in London at 9.30am, with the return departing at 7.15pm.

The stations on the new line to Cambridge were Melford (14 miles 60 chains from Marks Tey); Glemsford (17 miles 24 chains); Cavendish (18 miles 44 chains); Clare (21 miles 12 chains); Stoke (23 miles 23 chains); Sturmer (26 miles 18 chains); Haverhill (GE) (28 miles 18 chains); Withersfield Junction (30 miles 55 chains) (for freight only); Bartlow (34 miles 21 chains); Linton (36 miles 23 chains); and Abington (39 miles 2 chains). Shelford was 43 miles 13 chains from Marks Tey, and Cambridge was 46 miles 29 chains. On the line from Melford to Bury St. Edmunds, there was a station at Lavenham (19 miles 76 chains from Marks Tey); a goods siding at Cockfield (23 miles 18 chains), a station at Welnetham (26 miles 15 chains); another goods siding at Sicklesmere (about 27° miles); and a station at Bury East Gate (30 miles 30 chains), on the outskirts of Bury St. Edmunds. This branch joined the line from Haughley to Bury St. Edmunds at Bury Junction, 16 chains east of Bury St. Edmunds station and 30 miles 75 chains from Marks Tey. All the new lines, like the original Colchester, Stour Valley, Sudbury & Halstead Railway, were of single track, but designed to accommodate a double track if this were subsequently required.

Great Eastern Days

The Marks Tey-Sudbury line appears to have been provided with the electric telegraph as early as 1854, and was worked under the appropriate regulations in the ECR Rule Book, but without any form of train staff. On the other hand, the new lines were originally worked by train staff and ticket, but without any block telegraph. The staff stations were Sudbury, Melford, Clare, Haverhill, Bartlow and Shelford, on the Cambridge line; and Melford, Lavenham and Bury Junction, on the Bury St. Edmunds line.

In October, 1866, the passenger train service consisted of 4 trains in each direction on weekdays between Marks Tey and Sudbury, of which three ran through to and from Bury St. Edmunds. One of the latter was a mixed train from Sudbury to Bury. Between Sudbury and Cambridge, there were two weekday trains in each direction, both of which were mixed. There was also the goods train, previously mentioned, between Cambridge and Wivenhoe via the Colne Valley & Halstead Railway in each direction, and two goods trains each way between Sudbury and Marks Tey or Colchester. The Sunday service consisted of two passenger trains in each direction between Marks Tey and Bury St. Edmunds, and one in each direction between Sudbury and Cambridge.

By the spring of 1868, the Colne Valley freight train had been replaced by two freight trains each way between Sudbury and Cambridge, which ran through to and from Colchester or Marks Tey. There were also three passenger trains between Cambridge and Melford, two of which ran through to or from Sudbury. This section, however, now had no Sunday service. There were two freight trains in addition

Haverhill, looking north west in 1911. General view of goods shed and granary in front, Junction box on right. Short siding in front of granary shunted by tow rope or horse. Allen & Boggis (of Sudbury) coal depot on left. (Courtesy of National Railway Museum Windwood Collection)

between Marks Tey and Sudbury. On weekdays, there were four passenger trains between Colchester or Marks Tey and Sudbury, three of which ran through to or from Bury St. Edmunds. Two of these were mixed trains between Sudbury and Bury. The Sunday service consisted of two passenger trains between Marks Tey and Sudbury only.

By 1875, a coal and goods train was running through between Peterborough and Colchester via Cambridge and Sudbury, and the through running of such freight trains became a normal feature of the working on the Stour Valley line.

Interesting sidelights on the method of working are cast by the accounts of the two reported accidents during the 1870s, both on the Melford-Bury branch. The first one occurred on the 14th November, 1871, when a passenger train from Bury to Marks Tey was derailed at a pair of facing points at Welnetham station. The siding there, which was said to have been very seldom required, had been used on that day. The points had not been kept oiled, and the result that the balance weight had not acted properly in restoring them to their normal position after a horse-box had passed out of the siding, and the porter had forgotten to relock them. The report pointed out that it was desirable to interlock all facing points with signals on passenger lines. Fortunately, no-one was injured in the accident.

The second accident occurred on 9th August 1877, when the 1.05 p.m. passenger train from Colchester to Bury St. Edmunds via Sudbury ran into a ballast train standing at the branch home signal at Bury Junction. It was a fine afternoon, and the driver of the approaching passenger train had seen the branch junction home signal against him more than 1,000 yards away, but although the train was a light one of only five coaches, and was ascending a gradient of 1 in 100, he was unable, after again coming into view of the signal 250 yards away, to prevent his train colliding at slow speed with the brake van of the ballast train, which was 24 yards outside the home signal. The report blamed the passenger train driver for his negligence, the guard for sorting his parcels when he should have been observing his signals, the ballast train inspector for leaving his train standing outside the home signal when the passenger train was due, and the junction signalman for not sending the guard of the ballast train in time to recall it to be shunted clear. The report continued:

"Had the line been worked with the assistance of the block telegraph the collision would have been prevented, as the passenger train in that case would not have been allowed to leave East Gate station while the ballast train was standing outside

Long Melford 1911 view, looking north east. Maltings to the right (now luxury flats). GE covered vans in the siding, cattle vans in the foreground, and three tank wagons beyond the cattle pens – and a chicken coop in the middle of the yard. (Courtesy of National Railway Museum, Windwood Collection)

the junction signal. It would also no doubt have been prevented had the passenger train been fitted with an effective continuous brake under the control of the driver. Bury Junction required to be provided with a separate branch up distant signal visible from the cabin, instead of obtaining it as now by slotting the up home signal at East Gate station."

Initially there was no station at Cockfield but after a campaign by the local Rector, Reverend Richard Jeffreys and his curate, Reverend George Dobree, together with Thomas Jennings, a Newmarket racehorse trainer, who had then recently purchased Hall Farm in Cockfield, a passenger station was opened at Cockfield in November 1870. The Bury and Norwich Post of 15 November 1870 described the opening thus:

"A large party went from Bury, Lavenham, Melford and other places by the morning trains and on reaching Cockfield all were invited by Mr Jennings to a sumptuous champagne luncheon provided at his own house. The station itself was very prettily decorated with flags and the road from the station to the village was gay with similar adornments. The church bells rang out a merry peal and the inhabitants generally made holiday in honour of the occasion".

Sicklesmere siding was short-lived and had disappeared by 1875. On the Cambridge line, Abington station was renamed "Pampisford" on 1st May, 1875 and Melford was renamed "Long Melford" on 1st February, 1884. A siding at Cornard, 72 chains south of Sudbury, was opened during the seventies.

Following the disastrous single-line collision at Thorpe (near Norwich) on 10th September 1874, when 25 fatalities occurred, the GER hastened to extend train staff and ticket working to all of its single lines which were not already so worked, and the Marks Tey-Sudbury section was worked by this system from 26th October, 1874. The train staff stations were Marks Tey, Chappel and Sudbury.

In 1889, resignalling of the whole of the Stour Valley lines was put in hand, and by the end of 1890 block working was in force between Marks Tey and Long Melford Junction, and between Bury East Gate and Bury Junction. There were two signal boxes at Sudbury, named Sudbury Goods Junction and Sudbury Station; and also at Long Melford where the boxes were called Long Melford Station and Long Melford Junction respectively. (The Station Box at Long Melford was renamed Long Melford Yard by 1896.) The double line through each of these stations was worked by the double line block system between the boxes at each end.

By the end of 1892, the block system had been introduced throughout between Marks Tey, Shelford and Bury Junction. Signal boxes had been provided at all stations including Withersfield Siding, while Haverhill and Bartlow each had two boxes, the double lines through those stations being worked by the double line block system as in the cases of Sudbury and Long Melford. The signal boxes at Bures, Cockfield, Welnetham, Bury East Gate, Glemsford, Stoke, Sturmer, Withersfield Siding and Pampisford were not train staff stations. Cornard Siding possessed only a ground frame, worked by the level crossing keeper there. No trains normally called there, the siding's traffic requirements being usually met by a trip working from Sudbury

Marks Tey view west into station c1900 from overbridge, with the Stour Valley light diverging to the right. The Goods shed and water tank are in the right hand side, with the signal box centre. The main station building is on the up side at the left, a down train stands at the platform. The station signal box is at the apex between the main line and the Stour Valley line. The branch platform is occupied by a train, and a goods train headed by a Y14 is passing onto the Stour Valley from the down goods sidings. (Photograph courtesy of HMRS)

After the opening of the GER station at Haverhill, the passenger trains of the Colne Valley & Halstead Railway usually ran to and from the GE station, so as to make connections for Cambridge and other points on the Great Eastern line, and the Colne Valley station at Haverhill was eventually only used for the first passenger departure and the last arrival of the day, as well as for freight traffic.

By 1890, the Stour Valley lines were flourishing, so much so that an increase in accommodation was needed particularly at Chappel and Wakes Colne Station, and in February 1890 an estimate was received for 4 cottages for employees at an estimated cost of £900, which were built in November 1890. The signalling system and points were fully interlocked at a cost of £6,550 in April 1890, and it is believed that in this contract the signal box was erected on land owned by the Colne Valley and Halstead Railway, immediately resulting in litigation.

In August 1890 the footbridge was erected by J Westwood at a cost of £341.2.6d (£341.12^{1}/2p) and in November 1890 the new station buildings and goods shed were built by A Coe at a contract price of £2,990. It is believed that at this time the station buildings erected by the ECR were enlarged to form the Stationmaster's House.

A few years later, in 1894, the GER Way and Works Committee approved the expenditure of no less than £10.080 5s for the reconstruction of twenty seven bridges at various locations between Bury St Edmunds and Long Melford, and between Sudbury and Haverhill.

At this time between Marks Tey and Sudbury there were six passenger trains each way on weekdays and three on Sundays. The branch to Bury St. Edmunds had a service of five weekday trains each way, and there were four between Sudbury and Cambridge. Most of the passenger trains on weekdays ran through between Colchester or Marks Tey and Bury St. Edmunds or Cambridge. There was also a number of goods trains over all portions of the line, conveying coal, cattle, agricultural produce of all kinds, and general merchandise.

Withersfield siding was opened in 1891, and from the outset had a Saxby & Farmer built signalbox due to the demands of the Board of Trade at this time. It had a Duplex frame, and was to last until 1931 when it was replaced by a ground frame.

On Saturday 17th October, 1891, a serious accident occurred which no signalling installation could have avoided, when the 4.05 p.m. passenger train from Bury St. Edmunds to Marks Tey, hauled by 0-4-4 tank locomotive No. 169 (built by Neilson in 1873 to a Samuel Johnson design and subsequently rebuilt by Adams), was derailed whilst travelling at some speed on a curve between Lavenham and Long Melford. The train consisted of a guard's brake, five coaches and an empty horse box. The engine, which left the track first, turned completely over and lay with its wheels uppermost, while two of the six carriages fell on to their sides. Guard George Rampling was writing up his journal when the train was derailed, but he reacted quickly. Applying the Westinghouse brake prevented any telescoping, but could not stop three coaches plunging down a twelve foot embankment. After climbing out of his wrecked van, Rampling sent the fireman to protect the rear of the train, whilst he set off in an up direction even though he had suffered considerable head and leg injuries. On arrival at Long Melford Station he had a carriage attached to a goods engine to form a relief train.

Though none of the eight passengers was badly hurt, the sole first class passenger (a local JP) had suffered his second serious rail accident in five years. He had been reading *The Field* before his carriage was flung down the embankment. Afterwards he sat there in the reeds, "still reading and wondering what ever next". Despite being exhausted from the loss of blood, Rampling returned about 5.40 pm acting as the relief train's guard. On seeing his passengers finally arrive safely at Sudbury and some three hours after the accident, he set off to walk the two miles to his home, where he was eventually treated by a local doctor.

A considerable length of the single line track was ripped up and two locomotive wheels were broken. Two cranes were despatched from Cambridge, gangers worked all Saturday night, but one of the cranes over-reached itself and was also derailed

Bartlow Junction, showing the Audley End line on right and the Marks Tey line on left, June 1937 (Douglas Thompson, EARM collection)

requiring another crane from Stratford depot.

The Inspecting Officer found that the track was in good order, and that the accident had probably been caused by the engine, which was one of a class which ran unsteadily when driven chimney first. He stated that "the full load of coal and water, amounting to six tons, had been diminished by about $1^1/2$ tons, thereby reducing the weight on the bogie, which weight would be still further reduced by the forward wash of the water in the boiler on the falling gradient, down which the train was running. It is highly probably that the average speed between Lavenham and Long Melford of nearly 32 miles per hour was much exceeded, thus causing greater oscillation in the tank engine". The Inspector recommended the fitting of weights to the driving wheels, and the whole class was subsequently so fitted. No. 169 remained in service until 1907, and the whole class, which had been built in 1872-3, did not become extinct until 1912.

By 1896, electric tablet working had made its appearance on the line, having been installed between Bartlow and Shelford, all the intermediate signal boxes being tablet stations. This system was extended to the Marks Tey-Chappel section in 1900, and was installed between Sudbury and Clare by 1901. On the latter section, all the signal boxes except Glemsford were tablet stations.

Through the years the Colchester, Stour Valley, Sudbury & Halstead Railway company had continued to exist, but, since the GER worked the line and paid the rent regularly, the directors of the local company were (to quote 'Bradshaw's Manual')

Bury St Edmunds station in 1911, looking west. It includes the yard and station buildings, together with the maltings on the right hand side. The goods yard is in the left background. (Courtesy of the Historical Model Railway Society)

"chiefly occupied in distributing the proceeds". However, the Great Eastern Railway eventually reached an agreement with them to purchase the undertaking, and the purchase was sanctioned by the Great Eastern Railway (General Powers) Act (61 & 62 Vic. cap. lxvi), which received the Royal assent on 1st July 1898, on which date the old Stour Valley Railway Company ceased to exist.

By 1910 Marks Tey was served by a slip coach off the 5.05am service from Liverpool Street. Whilst it did convey passengers as far as Marks Tey (as there were no slip carriages without passenger accommodation) its prime purpose was to convey parcels, mails and newspapers for Stour Valley line stations. The carriage went forward as part of a Colchester to Peterborough via Haverhill goods train, departing Marks Tey at 7.10am – although this was altered to 6.40am in June 1910.

The period between this date and the First World War was the heyday of this, as of so many lines. Both passenger and goods traffic were plentiful, having regard to the wholly rural nature of the district, and the only station which failed to attract sufficient traffic to justify its existence was Bury East Gate, which was closed on 1st May, 1909. It did, however, re-open for two days in June 1914 when the Suffolk Agricultural Show was held at Bury St Edmunds. Throughout its life, it was a passenger only station with no freight facilities. The signal box at that station was also abolished.

In the summer of 1914, there were some seven weekday passenger trains in each direction between Marks Tey and Sudbury, six between Sudbury and Bury St.

COLCHESTER, CHAPPEL, LONG MELFORD, CAMBRIDGE, and BURY ST. EDMUNDS.—Great Eastern.

Miles	Down.	Week Days. mrn	mrn	mrn	mrn	mrn	aft	aft	aft	aft			Sundays. mrn	aft	aft
	Liverpool St., 288 London ..dep.	....	....	6 43	10 0	1145	2 22	4 18	5 30	7 12	....	....	9 10	3 40	4b15
—	Colchester....dep.	....	....	8 49	1055	1242	3 45	5 20	6 20	8 30	....	....	1019	....	7 12
5	Mark's Tey	....	....	9 15	1117	1 5	3 58	5 52	6 47	8 47	....	....	1041	5 6	7 33
8	Chappel .... arr.	....	....	9 22	1127	1 12	4 8	5 59	6 54	8 54	....	....	1049	5 14	7 41
	(below) dep.	....	....	9 24	1129	1 14	4 11	6 2	6 56	8 57	....	....	1051	5 16	7 43
12	Bures	....	....	9 32	1137	1 22	4 19	6 10	7 5	9 5	....	....	11 0	5 25	7 52
16½	Sudbury .. arr.	....	....	9 40	1146	1 30	4 27	6 18	7 13	9 13	....	....	11 9	5 34	8 1
	dep.	7 15	7 32	9 43	1149	1 34	4 30	6 27	7 15	....	....	....	....	....	....
19½	Long Melford arr.	7 22	7 39	9 49	1155	1 40	4 36	6 33	7 21	....	....	....	....	....	....
—	Long Melford dp	7 23	....	9 56	1158	....	4 42	6 36	....	....	....	....	....	....	....
22¾	Glemsford	7 29	....	10 2	12 8	....	4 49	6 43	....	....	....	....	....	....	....
23¾	Cavendish	7 33	....	10 6	12 7	....	4 53	6 47	....	....	....	....	....	....	....
26¼	Clare ‡	7 41	....	1012	1213	....	5 1	6 54	....	....	....	....	....	....	....
28¾	Stoke	7 46	....	1017	1218	....	5 7	7 0	....	....	....	....	....	....	....
31¼	Sturmer	7 52	....	1023	1224	....	5 14	7 7	....	....	....	....	....	....	....
33¾	Haverhill	7 59	....	1030	1232	....	5 28	7 16	....	....	....	....	....	....	....
38¾	Bartlow 297	8 11	....	1042	1243	....	5 40	7 28	....	....	....	....	....	....	....
41¼	Linton	8 16	....	1047	1248	....	5 45	7 34	....	....	....	....	....	....	....
43¾	Pampisford	8 22	....	1056	1254	....	5 51	7 40	....	....	....	....	....	....	....
48¼	Shelford 298	8 31	....	11 5	1 4	....	6 2	7 50	....	....	....	....	....	....	....
100½	298 London * ar.	1015	....	1240	2 49	....	8 26	9 57	....	....	....	....	....	....	....
51½	Cambdge 296 ar	8 37	....	1111	1 12	....	6 10	7 58	....	....	....	....	....	....	....
—	Long Melford dep.	....	7 41	1020	12 4	1 42	4 51	....	7 23	....	....	....	....	....	....
25	Lavenham	....	7 57	1032	1215	1 52	5 1	....	7 33	....	....	....	....	....	....
28½	Cockfield .... [305	....	8 5	1039	1222	1 59	5 8	....	7 40	....	....	....	....	....	....
31½	Welnetham .. [300	....	8 12	1045	1228	2 5	5 14	....	7 46	....	....	....	....	....	....
36½	Bury St. Edmunds a	....	8 23	1054	1237	2 14	5 22	....	7 56	....	....	....	....	....	....

Miles	Up.	Week Days. mrn	mrn	mrn	aft	aft	aft	aft	aft			Sundays. mrn	aft	aft
	Bury St. Edmunds	7 34	9 21	1112	2 30	4 5	....	5 43	....	....	....	....	....	....
5	Welnetham	7 43	9 30	1121	2 38	4 14	....	5 53	....	....	....	....	....	....
7¾	Cockfield	7 49	9 35	1127	2 45	4 20	....	5 59	....	....	....	....	....	....
11¼	Lavenham	7 55	9 42	1134	2 52	4 28	....	6 7	....	....	....	....	....	....
16¼	Long Melford arr.	8 5	9 52	1144	3 3	4 38	....	6 18	....	....	....	....	....	....
—	Cambridge dp	....	8 58	1049	1 45	....	4 47	....	7 10	....	....	....	....	....
—	296 Londn* .d	....	5 33	8 40	12 0	....	2 35	....	5 12	....	....	....	....	....
—	3¼ Shelford	....	9 5	1047	1 52	....	4 54	....	7 18	....	....	....	....	....
—	7¼ Pampisford	....	9 13	1055	2 0	....	5 2	....	7 26	....	....	....	....	....
—	10¼ Linton	....	9 20	11 2	2 6	....	5 9	....	7 35	....	....	....	....	....
—	12¾ Bartlow 297	....	9 25	11 7	2 11	....	5 14	....	7 40	....	....	....	....	....
—	18¼ Haverhill	....	9 40	1120	2 24	....	5 28	....	7 55	....	....	....	....	....
—	20¼ Sturmer	....	9 45	1125	2 29	....	5 33	....	8 0	....	....	....	....	....
—	22¾ Stoke	....	9 51	1131	2 35	....	5 39	....	8 6	....	....	....	....	....
—	25¼ Clare ‡	....	9 57	1137	2 41	....	5 45	....	8 13	....	....	....	....	....
—	27¾ Cavendish	....	10 6	1143	2 47	....	5 51	....	8 19	....	....	....	....	....
—	29¼ Glemsford	....	1010	1147	2 51	....	5 55	....	8 24	....	....	....	....	....
—	31¼ Long Melford	....	1015	1152	2 56	....	6 0	....	8 29	....	....	....	....	....
—	Long Melford dep	8 7	1018	1158	3 7	4 44	6 2	6 20	8 31	....	....	....	....	....
19½	Sudbury ... arr.	8 13	1024	12 4	3 13	4 50	6 8	6 26	8 37	....	....	....	....	....
	dep.	8 15	1027	12 8	3 17	4 52		6 30	8 39	....	....	9 25	4 28	6 42
24¼	Bures	8 24	1036	1217	3 26	5 1		6 39	8 48	....	....	9 34	4 37	6 51
28¼	Chappel .... arr.	8 32	1044	1225	3 34	5 9		6 47	8 56	....	....	9 42	4 45	6 59
—	(below) dep.	8 34	1048	1227	3 38	5 11		6 55	8 57	....	....	9 44	4 46	7 5
31¼	Mark's Tey 292	8 43	1056	1235	3 45	5 18		7 2	9 4	....	....	9 53	4 54	7 12
36¼	Colchester † 310 ar	9 7	11 8	1 3	4 0	5 32		7 17	9 15	....	....	10 7	5 13	....
78	292 London* .. arr.	1010	1227	2 25	5 48	....		9 8	....	....	....	1230	....	8 52

b Via Colchester. * Liverpool Street. † Station for Nayland (5½ miles). ‡ Station for Denston (5½ miles).

For OTHER TRAINS between Colchester and Mark's Tey, see pages 288 to 295; between Shelford and Cambridge, see pages 296 to 299.

SAXMUNDHAM and ALDEBURGH.—Great Eastern.

Miles	Down.	Week Days. mrn	mrn	mrn	mrn	mrn (Weds. & Sats.)	aft	aft	aft	Sndys aft	
	Liverpool Street, 288 London ......dep.	5 5	....	8 33	10 0	11 45	3 25	5 0	....	4 15	....
—	Saxmundham ......dep.	8 1	9 42	1125	1253	2 58	6 6	7 25	8 16	7 6	....
4	Leiston	8 12	9 51	1135	1 3	3 8	6 17	7 35	8 28	7 16	....
6½	Aldeburgh ......arr.	8 24	....	1145	1 13	3 18	6 27	7 45	8 40	7 26	....

Miles	Up.	Week Days. mrn	mrn	mrn	mrn	aft (Weds. & Sats.)	aft (Except Sats.)	aft (Sats.)	aft	Sn aft
	Aldeburgh ......dep.	6 57	8 50	....	1153	2 23	4 25	4 37	6 53	6 32
4¼	Leiston	7 9	9 0	9 57	12 3	2 33	4 35	4 47	7 3	6 42
8¾	Saxmundham 288, 292 arr.	7 20	9 9	10 6	1212	2 42	4 44	4 56	7 12	6 51
99¼	292 London (Liverpool St.) arr	1033	1135	....	3 30	6 0	8 5	8 15	....	10 3

CHAPPEL, HALSTEAD, and HAVERHILL.—Colne Valley and Halstead.

Miles	Down.	Week Days. mrn	mrn (Mons. and Sats.)	mrn	mrn (Saturdays.)	aft	aft (Saturdays.)	aft	aft	Sundays. mrn	aft	
	Liverpool Street Station, London ......dep.	6 43	6 43	10 0	1145	2 22	4 18	5 30	7 12	9 10	4b15	....
—	Chappel ......dep.	9 25	9 25	1132	1 18	4 15	6 5	6 58	9 2	1053	7 45	....
2	White Colne	9 30	9 30	1137	1 23	4 20	6 10	7 3	9 7	1058	7 50	....
3½	Earls Colne	9 33	9 33	1140	1 26	4 23	6 13	7 6	9 10	11 1	7 53	....
6	Halstead	9 41	9 41	1148	1 34	4 31	6 22	7 14	9 18	11 9	8 1	....
9½	Sible & Castle Hedingham	9 49	9 49	1156	1 42	4 39	6 31	7 22	9s26	1117	8 9	....
12	Yeldham	....	10 7	12 3	1 49	4 46	6 38	7 29	9s33	1124	8 16	....
16½	Birdbrook	....	1018	1214	2 0	4 57	6 49	7 40	9s44	1135	8 27	....
19½	Haverhill ......arr.	....	1025	1222	2 8	5 5	6 57	7 48	9s52	1143	8 35	....

Miles	Up.	Week Days. mrn	mrn	mrn (Saturdays only.)	aft	aft	aft (Saturdays only.)	Sundays. mrn	aft	
	Haverhill ......dep.	7c38	9 45	1125	2 40	5 48	7 58	8 48	5 58	....
3¼	Birdbrook	7c47	9 54	1134	2 49	5 57	8 7	8 57	6 9	....
7½	Yeldham	7c56	10 5	1144	2 58	6 6	8 16	9 6	6 19	....
10¼	Sible & Castle Hedingham	8 3	1012	1152	3 5	6 13	8 23	9 13	6 27	....
13¾	Halstead	8 12	1021	12 3	3 14	6 22	8 32	9 22	6 37	....
16	Earls Colne	8 20	1029	12 8	3 22	6 30	8 40	9 30	6 48	....
17½	White Colne..	8 24	1033	1210	3 26	6 34	8 44	9 34	6 53	....
19½	Chappel (above) ....arr.	8 30	1039	1220	3 32	6 40	8 50	9 40	7 0	....
69½	London * ......arr.	1010	1227	2 25	5 48	9 8	....	1230	8 52	....

b Via Colchester. *c* Mondays and Saturdays. *s* Saturdays only. * Liverpool Street Station.

Edmunds and five between Sudbury and Cambridge. These included through trains between Cambridge and Clacton via Sudbury and Colchester in each direction for holiday-makers. In this summer too, there was a Sunday service of two trains in each direction between Colchester or Marks Tey and Cambridge, and two between Sudbury and Bury St. Edmunds, while there were four altogether between Marks Tey and Sudbury. Through carriages worked between Liverpool Street and Sudbury on four trains in each direction on weekdays; Colne Valley trains conveyed through carriages to or from Colchester, which were attached to or detached from GER trains at Chappel.

Freight traffic too, was heavy. There were through trains between March or Peterborough, on the one hand, and Wickford, Brentwood or Aldersbrook (near Ilford) on the other, running via Bury St. Edmunds, Sudbury and Marks Tey, this route being mainly although not entirely, preferred to the Cambridge line for through trains, as it entailed a shorter stretch of single line and avoided the very steeply-graded section between Haverhill and Bartlow. These trains involved the line between Marks Tey and Bury being kept open throughout the night.

The outbreak of war in 1914 bought little diminution in traffic, and in 1916 further installations of the electric tablet system were made between Chappel and Sudbury, and between Long Melford and Bury St. Edmunds. On the former section

Sudbury station approach & north signal box 1911 view southwards from signal post. Down refuge line with trap on right hand side. (Courtesy of the Historical Model Railway Society)

Bures became a tablet station, but as the station only possessed a single platform, and the loop was only signalled for goods trains, two passenger trains could not cross each other there. On the Bury St. Edmunds branch, Welnetham signal box was not a block post and Cockfield, although a tablet station, was not a crossing place. The only sections of the Stour Valley line still worked by the train staff and ticket system were those between Clare and Haverhill Junction and between Haverhill Station and Bartlow. A minor alteration at this time was the renaming of Chappel station as "Chappel & Wakes Colne" from 1st October, 1914.

The last serious accident on the Stour Valley line, but one which, unhappily caused a fatal casualty, occurred in the early morning of 29th November, 1919. The 6.47 a.m. train from Sudbury to Cambridge arrived at Haverhill at 7.26 a.m., at which time the 5.30 a.m. Cambridge to Long Melford goods train was standing on the main line. The morning was dark and stormy, with sleet falling. When the goods train drew forward into the up platform, the signalman at Haverhill Station Box, which was at the Cambridge end of the up platform, took the train staff from the driver, "cleared" for the goods and obtained permission for the passenger train to proceed towards Bartlow. Then, without setting the points or signals for the passenger train to leave, the signalman left his box, took the train staff to the driver, and then walked down the platform to where the guard was standing, telling him that if time was up he might go. The guard thereupon showed his green light to the driver, who failed to notice that the starting signal was at danger, and started the train, which, as the points were not set for the single line, ran into a siding. The engine was running tender first, and a piece of sacking was fastened between the cab roof and the tender as protection from the weather. By the time the driver realised where he was, it was impossible for him to prevent the train colliding with the buffers. The rear compartment of the first carriage and the leading compartment of the second were smashed in, and a passenger was killed.

LNER Regime

On 1st January, 1923, under the grouping system prescribed by the Railways Act, 1921, the Great Eastern Railway became part of the new London & North Eastern Railway; the Colne Valley and Halstead Railway, as one of the companies became part of the LNER on 1st July, 1923. The Colne Valley station at Haverhill was closed to passenger traffic on 14th July 1924, but remained open to freight, and on 1st February, 1925, was renamed Haverhill South, while the former GER station became Haverhill North. Within a few years, distant signals on the line began to have their red lamp-glasses changed to orange, and their arms painted in the now familiar yellow and black, while upper quadrant signals made their first appearance.

In the years following the war, road competition began to make itself felt, and several economies were affected in operating the Stour Valley line. In common with many other rural lines, the signalling was re-examined with a view to economies being made. At the end of 1925, Pampisford ceased to be a crossing place and block station and the signal-box was replaced by ground frames. Originally there were three signalboxes at Marks Tey, but rationalisation came here with both Marks Tey Junction and Marks Tey East signalboxes closing in 1925. In 1926, Bartlow Station and Welnetham signalboxes were abolished. In the former case, the working at the south end of the station was transferred to Bartlow Junction box, while Welnetham box was replaced by a ground frame. In October, 1931, electric tablet working was installed between Bartlow and Haverhill North Station, and between Haverhill North Junction and Clare. The intermediate signal boxes at Stoke and Sturmer were abolished and replaced by ground frames. On 16th July, 1933, Haverhill North Station box was abolished and the working transferred to the Junction box. A scheme for rationalisation of the signalling at Sudbury and Long Melford was authorised on 27 October 1932 at a cost of £3,532. On 9 April 1934 the nineteen lever Sudbury Station box was abolished and the work transferred to Sudbury Goods Junction box: both of these boxes dated from 1889 when the station was interlocked by Saxby & Farmer. Around the same time, Long Melford Yard signalbox was closed and the work transferred to Long Melford Junction. On 1st January, 1937, Withersfield Siding was closed, but was reopened on 1st November, 1943, though without a signal box.

Despite road competition, however, there was still a fair quantity of traffic, and during the thirties the train service underwent little alteration. In 1937, for example, there were five weekday trains each way between Sudbury and Cambridge of which in the down direction, four ran through from Colchester, and indeed one of these started from Brightlingsea, one from Clacton, and one from Harwich. Two of the up trains ran through to Colchester, and one to Marks Tey, one of the Colchester

Marks Tey station in 1930 (Douglas Thompson, EARM collection)

Sturmer station in June 1937 (EARM collection)

trains being extended to Clacton during August.

From Bury St. Edmunds, there was one train which ran through to Marks Tey, one to Harwich and one to Colchester, while there were three trains to Long Melford with an additional one on Wednesdays. In the opposite direction, there were six trains from Long Melford to Bury St. Edmunds, of which one originated from Sudbury, one from Marks Tey, and one from Colchester. An evening train in each direction between Sudbury and Colchester completed the weekday passenger service, apart from a Saturday afternoon train from Marks Tey which ran through via Chappel onto the Colne Valley line. In all other cases, traffic to and from the Colne Valley at this time was catered for by through carriages to and from Marks Tey or Colchester, which were attached to or detached from the Stour Valley line trains at Chappel.

Through carriages between Liverpool Street and Sudbury were not reinstated after the First World War, except for a slip carriage which was detached at Marks Tey from the 4.57 p.m. Liverpool Street to Clacton train, and which was then attached to a train for Bury St. Edmunds via Sudbury, being returned to London in the morning. This was the last slip carriage working on the LNER or indeed any railway other than the GWR. It did not operate during the summer months, when the main line train stopped at Marks Tey instead of slipping, and finally ceased after 1st July, 1939.

A number of through long-distance excursion trains ran via the Stour Valley line between various Midland towns and Clacton or Walton-on-the-Naze during the summer months, and there were also four through freight trains from Colchester to

Whitemoor via Cambridge or Bury St. Edmunds. The chief of these was the 6.00 p.m. No. 1 Braked Goods from St. Botolphs to Whitemoor, which was usually known to the staff as "the Vacuum", and was normally worked by an ex-GN class K2 2-6-0. This train originally ran via Cambridge, but by the summer of 1939 was running via Bury.

During the Summer, too, there were a number of excursion trains serving local stations, affording facilities for a day at the sea or in London. They also included evening excursions to Southend, Clacton, Walton or Liverpool Street, arriving back at the Stour Valley stations in the small hours of the morning. Extremely cheap fares were charged for these trains, the evening excursion return fare from Bures to Liverpool Street, for example, being 2/8d (14p). There were also regular Sunday half-day excursions from Liverpool Street to Bury St. Edmunds, serving the Stour Valley line stations en route.

Locomotives to be seen on the line included the J15 0-6-0s, E4 2-4-0s, the various classes of 2-4-2 tanks and the "Claud Hamilton" 4-4-0s which had been seen since GER days, together with the occasional B12 4-6-0s, the large J17, J19, J20 and J21 0-6-0s, as well as standard LNER J39 0-6-0s and ex-GNR K2 2-6-0s on "the Vacuum". Some ex-G.N. 4-4-0s were also tried on the line, these including Nos. 3052, 3055, 3056, 4366 and 4372. Perhaps the most historically interesting locomotives to be seen in these years however, were the class D13 survivors - these last remaining examples of the 4-4-0 rebuilds of the old GER class T19. These engines, Nos. 8023, 8035 and 8039 lasted until 1943-44.

At the outbreak of the Second World War in September 1939, the passenger service was drastically reduced, but the freight service remained unaltered at first. An interesting working which commenced on 30th October, 1939 and continued until 26th October 1940 was a parcels train from Sudbury to Colchester, conveying vans detached from a passenger train from Bury St. Edmunds. From 2nd October 1939, the "Vacuum" Braked Goods train to Whitemoor started direct from Marks Tey, and continued to do so throughout the rest of its existence; on 3rd February, 1941, two additional through freight trains from Whitemoor to Parkeston and Colchester began to run via Bury St. Edmunds and the Stour Valley line.

The most interesting wartime regular passenger working was the through train in each direction between Liverpool Street and Sudbury, which began to run on 9th October, 1943. For many years, even in G.E.R. days, a through passenger train from Liverpool Street to Bury St. Edmunds via Sudbury had run on the day preceding Bank Holiday week-ends, but now the 2.15 p.m. Liverpool Street to Sudbury train commenced to run every Saturday, returning from Sudbury to Liverpool Street at 5.25 p.m. on Sunday evenings and preceding by only 10 minutes the ordinary passenger train from Sudbury to Marks Tey. Moreover, the London train was allowed a stop of two minutes at Bures, so that, if the local train started punctually from Sudbury, it was inevitably delayed at Bures until the through train had cleared the long section to Chappel. With some subsequent alterations in timing, this through train ran throughout the remainder of the war and indeed was not finally discontinued until 30th September, 1950. This train, which of course, had to

Two photos at Clare from the camera of Dr Ian C Allen: the top view shows B1 61046 in the yard. The lower scene shows B17 61622 departing on a freight. Photographs courtesy of The Transport Treasury

reverse at Marks Tey, was usually hauled by a rebuilt B12 4-6-0 on the main line, and a "Claud Hamilton" 4-4-0 between Marks Tey and Sudbury. In its last post-war days, it was a third-class only train, composed of an eight coach, non-corridor suburban set – not the most comfortable accommodation for a ride of over 58 miles!

It is interesting to note that for many years reversal at Marks Tey was necessary even for trains from Colchester to the Stour Valley line, as there was no facing crossover at Marks Tey to give direct access to the branch. This situation was not rectified until early in the Second World War, when the necessary facing crossover was installed.

As the war progressed, the line became busier, particularly after the allied bomber offensive had begun and when both British and American aerodromes had been established throughout East Anglia. Special trains were run between Cambridge and Chappel, conveying rubble for the construction of a new aerodrome at Wormingford, and when this had been built and brought into use, a petrol depot was provided at Chappel. Two trains ran daily from Cambridge to Chappel with high-octane petrol for the aircraft, returning empty to Cambridge. There were some heart-stopping moments for signalmen and trainmen whenever one of these petrol trains happened to be stopped at a signalbox at a time when enemy aircraft or a "flying bomb" was overhead!

During World War Two, rail served oil storage tanks were built at Chappel & Wakes Colne, which are clearly shown here with E4 62792 on an unidentified working. (Dr Ian C Allen, courtesy of The Transport Treasury)

From 15th February, 1944, the line between Bury St. Edmunds and Marks Tey again began to be open all night for the running of additional freight trains between March, Whitemoor and Colchester or Marks Tey, and the signalmen worked twelve-hour shifts. The value of the line as a through route was also utilised for the running of a number of special troop trains between Eastern Counties stations and the North or West of England. The line figured prominently, too, in various evacuation plans, although fortunately, only the original scheme, for the evacuation of schoolchildren form London in 1939, ever had to be implemented.

Increasing passenger traffic resulted in a strengthening of some of the passenger trains, and those which comprised both a Stour Valley and a Colne Valley portion often consisted of nine coaches between Marks Tey and Chappel – a heavy task for a little E4 2-4-0, struggling manfully to keep time. It therefore became more the practice for the Colne Valley trains to run independently from the Stour Valley trains between Marks Tey and Chappel, and this practice continued for many cases for the remainder of the existence of the Colne Valley passenger service.

W.D. "Austerity" 2-8-0 locomotives appeared on many of the through freight trains, including the 8.45 p.m. Marks Tey to Whitemoor, which had now been downgraded to a Class A unfitted freight train. As on many lines, especially in the eastern and southern counties, the train working was subject to frequent dislocation and delay by air-raid warnings, although no actual damage was done, and the through

Ivatt Class 2MT 46467 pauses at Bures on a local service, date unknown. Photo by B.D.J. Walsh

Cavendish station. Photo by B.D.J. Walsh

freight trains in particular were sometimes wildly late – to the extent, on occasions, of several hours. However, they always got through to their destinations and performed an essential service in transporting the massive quantities of materials required for the war effort.

Peacetime and Nationalisation

After the cessation of hostilities, the line reverted to its peacetime services. Through excursion trains were run over the Stour Valley and the Colne Valley lines at summer weekends, mostly to Clacton, and there were also excursion workings from local stations to seaside resorts and to London.

In the summer of 1954, a regular through express began to run on Saturdays in each direction between Leicester and Clacton via Cambridge and Sudbury, and it continued to run each summer until the end of the summer of 1966. In the summer of 1959, too, a through express ran between Sheffield and Clacton, via Bury St. Edmunds and Sudbury on Saturdays only. During this period, the Sunday service included not only the stopping trains between Marks Tey and Sudbury, but also a train in each direction between Sudbury and Clacton and between Cambridge and

Cockfield station on 18th September 1953 (Douglas Thompson, EARM collection)

Clacton via the Colne Valley line. All these through trains were normally hauled by "Sandringham" 4-6-0 locomotives of class B17 (or the rebuilds of class B2) until their replacement by Brush diesel locomotives. Apart from the "Sandringhams" and the Ivatt 2-6-0s which made their appearance from 1951, the line continued to be worked almost exclusively by the same ex-GER locomotives types as had performed such stalwart service for so many years. Indeed, in the remaining days of steam, the line presented a decidedly Great Eastern atmosphere. Its stations were mostly of typical Great Eastern design, the only exceptions being those at Chappel and Bures, which were both original Colchester, Stour Valley, Sudbury & Halstead Railway structures. The old GER blue-painted station name-boards survived in many cases until the late 'fifties before being replaced by BR standard boards, and one of the former – that from Welnetham – is now part of the National Railway Museum collection at York. Lower quadrant signals of GER design were to be seen in some numbers, and survived on the line north of Sudbury until final closure. The modern innovations on the line, in fact, seemed by their very contrast to emphasise the older features, while when one travelled (as was still possible in the early 'fifties) in a gas-lit clerestory-roofed carriage, hauled by an old Holden engine, through small stations still lit by oil lamps, one could well imagine oneself back in the Golden Age of Railways. This impression was heightened, too, by the countryside through which the line passed. With its picturesque farmland, reminiscent of Constable's pictures, and the old villages of rural Suffolk, it provided tranquillity and calm more in keeping with Victorian England than with the bustle of modern times. The train working however, was by no means devoid of liveliness. Although the line followed, for the most part, the course of the River Stour and other rivers, there were some very severe gradients in the intervening sections. These necessitated some very heavy locomotive work on the up-grades and, on the down-grades, speed which, although nominally limited to 50 m.p.h., could nevertheless be exhilarating over a sharply curved stretch. The writer well remembers riding in the first carriage of a train which rocketed down from Withersfield Siding towards Haverhill behind a Holden E4 2-4-0 at no less than 59 m.p.h. - an awe-inspiring experience! This tradition of high speed on this particular stretch was certainly not abandoned in the diesel days, and within a few weeks of the final closure of the Cambridge – Sudbury line, the writer recorded a speed of over 70 m.p.h. in a diesel multiple-unit train on the way down to Haverhill.

Modernisation & Contraction

More drastic changes on the line, however, were soon to be made. On 1st January, 1959, diesel multiple-units and diesel rail-buses took over the local Stour and Colne Valley services, and in order to utilise the multiple-units to the maximum extent, some of them ran through between Ipswich or Norwich and Cambridge via Marks Tey and the Stour Valley line. As all these trains stopped at all stations, however, a journey from Norwich to Cambridge by this route was apt to be a tedious business except to the railway enthusiast!

Increasing road competition and rising costs began to bite deeply into the economy of the line, especially on the freight side. The old-established 8.45 p.m. Marks Tey to Whitemoor ran for the last time on 31st October 1959, and by 18th June 1962 vanished from the Stour Valley Line, leaving only the local trains, now, of course, diesel-hauled.

Meanwhile, the first passenger service casualties had occurred. The passenger service between Long Melford and Bury St. Edmunds, which had become very sparse, was finally withdrawn on and from 10th April 1961, although a Rambler's Special ran from Liverpool Street to Bury St. Edmunds and back via Long Melford on 4th June 1961, and two special trains for the wedding of Patrick Wolrige-Gordon MP ran from Liverpool Street to Lavenham and back via Cambridge and Bury St. Edmunds on 2nd June 1962. The Lavenham to Long Melford section was dismantled in 1962. Then the passenger service on the Colne Valley line was withdrawn on and from 1st January 1962. On the Bury line, the remaining freight service operated only between Bury and Lavenham, while on the Colne Valley line, it ran between Chappel and Yeldham. Sturmer station was closed to freight traffic on 25th June 1962.

There was then a lull for two years, after which the decline was more rapid. Welnetham station was closed to freight traffic on 13th July 1964, as was Chappel & Wakes Colne, the Colne Valley freight trains continuing to run through to and from Marks Tey. Apart from these, the only freight train on the line south of Sudbury was

Sun and shadow in Chappel Cutting: afternoon Colchester to Whitemoor freight, drawn by J17 65539 on 15 June 1957 (G.R. Mortimer)

a train which ran daily, if required, from Sudbury to Bures and back and which ceased when freight facilities were withdrawn from Bures on 28th December 1964. On the same day, Cavendish and Bartlow, as well as three Colne Valley line stations - White Colne, Earls Colne and Yeldham - also lost their freight facilities. As another Colne Valley station - Sible & Castle Hedingham - had been closed to freight traffic on 13th July 1964, the Colne Valley trains only ran now between Marks Tey and Halstead, the station at Haverhill South being served by trips from Haverhill North.

On 19th April 1965, the Bury St. Edmunds – Lavenham freight service was withdrawn and that line was closed entirely, together with Cockfield and Lavenham stations. On the same day a similar fate overtook the Colne Valley line, including Haverhill South, and Withersfield Siding, Stoke, Pampisford and Shelford were also closed to freight traffic. The signal box at Bures, now not required for freight traffic or for crossing purposes, was abolished on 6th September 1965.

There was now merely a freight service between Cambridge, Linton, Haverhill North, Clare, Glemsford, Long Melford, and Sudbury, together with the passenger service between Colchester, Marks Tey and Cambridge, serving all the intermediate stations on the line. In order to economise in passenger service operation, conductor guards had been introduced on 28th January 1963, and all stations on the line except

CONDUCTOR GUARD WORKING
CAMBRIDGE – COLCHESTER
AUDLEY END – BARTLOW LINE

Commencing on 28th January, 1963 passenger booking facilities will be withdrawn from the undermentioned stations and tickets will be issued and collected on trains by the Guard

PAMPISFORD
LINTON
BARTLOW
STURMER
STOKE
CLARE
CAVENDISH
GLEMSFORD
LONG MELFORD
BURES
CHAPPEL and WAKES COLNE

In addition passenger booking facilities will be withdrawn from
HAVERHILL and
SAFFRON WALDEN
on Sundays only
with effect from 3rd February, 1963

If the Guard is unable to issue a throughout ticket to destination, directions will be given to passengers regarding the station at which re-booking will be necessary

Season tickets normally issued from the above stations should be obtained through the Station Masters at Haverhill or Sudbury who will also deal with arrangements for Passengers Luggage in Advance

Concurrent with the change in booking arrangements parcels traffic will cease to be accepted at PAMPISFORD, STURMER and STOKE

Railbus from the Audley End branch on the left, accelerates smartly for Haverhill at Bartlow Junction where it changed direction. 29th August 1964 (G.R.Mortimer)

Sudbury and Haverhill North became unstaffed halts.

Mention may be made in passing of the branch from Audley End, on the Cambridge main line, through Saffron Walden to Bartlow, which was also closed entirely on 19th April 1965. Opened to Bartlow by the Saffron Walden Railway on 22nd October 1866, it was worked by the GER from the beginning and was absorbed by the latter company on 1st January 1877. Although it had a connection with the Stour Valley line at the north end of Bartlow station, its passenger trains used an entirely separate platform there, connected with the Stour Valley platforms by means of a footpath. Apart from a few freight trains which ran through from the branch to Cambridge via Bartlow and Shelford, and one or two passenger services which ran through between Haverhill and the branch in 1914 and again in the last few years of the passenger service, there was no through working on to the Stour Valley line. The passenger service was withdrawn on 7th September 1964.

In April 1965, the British Railways Board applied to the East Anglian Transport Users' Consultative Committee for permission to withdraw the passenger service from the whole of the Stour Valley line from Marks Tey to Cambridge. This proposal aroused strenuous opposition, and at the Committee's hearing of objections at Sudbury Town Hall in August 1965, there was a bitter and protracted struggle. In

(top) Horseheath cutting and bridge: rear of Cambridge to Sudbury train on 5th September 1964. (Lower) 8.55am Cambridge to Clacton climbing two miles after Bartlow, headed by D5583, on 22nd August 1964 (both by G. R. Mortimer)

the result, announced on 2nd November 1965, the Committee granted permission for the withdrawal of the passenger service between Sudbury and Cambridge, but refused permission for the closure of the Marks Tey – Sudbury section on account of its use by commuters and by weekend traffic and because of the growth of Sudbury. British Rail demanded a subsidy of £26,000 in 1966 to keep the line open for a further twelve months, but whilst this was being considered by the local authorities BR announced on 25th January 1967 that the amount required would be doubled to £52,000 as they had found that the track was in poor condition and needed substantial repairs. This caused the local authorities to withdraw their opposition to the proposed closure.

As a further economy, both Sudbury and Haverhill became unstaffed halts on and from 14th August 1966. On 12th September of that year, freight facilities were withdrawn from Long Melford, Glemsford, Clare and Linton, leaving only Haverhill North and Sudbury served by the daily freight service from Cambridge. This was itself withdrawn on 31st October 1966, and the withdrawal of the passenger service between Sudbury and Cambridge on 6th March 1967 marked the complete closure of the line north of Sudbury, which has now been lifted. The signal box at Chappel was taken out of use on 20th August 1967, and the loop and all points removed, while the

The 1347 Cambridge to Sudbury calling at Stoke on 2nd November 1966: the nearer Cravens unit is in dark green, the other car in the then rare rail blue. (G.R. Mortimer)

layout at Sudbury was reduced to a single line serving the former up platform. This left only the original branch of 1849 which carries a shuttle service of diesel multiple-unit trains. In fact, it had been proposed to close the existing Sudbury station and to re-adapt the site of the original one-platform terminus for passenger use once more, but that scheme has never been implemented as originally planned.

Shortly before the withdrawal of passenger services between Sudbury and Colchester came a rather bizarre working, albeit not one available for public use. As part of a test of a new mileage ingredient in their petrol, Shell Mex fitted a brand new Vauxhall Cresta car with rail wheels, radio control equipment and a glass petrol tank – this designed to give greater visible impact during the filming. It was perceived that this would give more accurate test results as unlike a road test the gradients were generally less severe and the car would also have a clear run without any potential traffic hold-ups.

The tests were originally planned to take place on Sundays 27th November, 4th, 11th and 18th December 1966. However these were postponed and it was not until Thursday 5th January 1967 that the car was delivered to Haverhill Goods Yard and the rail wheels were fitted. On Sunday 8th January a trial run with the car coupled to a DMU was carried out to ensure that there were no problems: after this it was decided to change the car's wheels for a different sort. Further tests took place on the following Sunday, 15th January, which were deemed satisfactory and

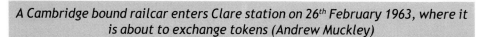

A Cambridge bound railcar enters Clare station on 26th February 1963, where it is about to exchange tokens (Andrew Muckley)

Two views at Haverhill in 1967 by G.R. Mortimer: the top shows the 1055 Cambridge to Sudbury on closing day, 4th March. The lower shows the 1230 Cambridge to Sudbury approaching the station on 21st January.

the official test with members of the RAC present to oversee the operations took place on 22nd January. Having one gallon of fuel in the tank, the car ran from Shelford before running out between Sudbury station and the signal box. It was then hauled back, refilled with another gallon – but this time with the new mileage ingredient – for a second run. This departed from Shelford at 10.30am and ran out of fuel just short of Bures station, indicating that the mileage ingredient lived up to its claims. The following Sunday – 29th January – saw the actual filming take place, from both the ground and from a helicopter.

The Line since contraction

In November 1968, the British Railways Board again published proposals for the closure of the remaining portion of the Stour Valley line, consequent upon the decision of the Minister of Transport not to continue its subsidy. Again severe opposition was aroused and at the Committee's meeting at Sudbury Town Hall in July 1969, the proposals were strongly contested. Until June 1972, neither the Committee nor the Minister announced any decision on the matter, but the Minister for the Environment stated that the line would close in July 1974, if the local authorities did not support further continuation of the service. At this stage the Stour Valley Railway Preservation Society forwarded proposals to British Rail to operate a privately owned rail service on closure

B1 61287 on track lifting between Lavenham and Long Melford in May 1962.
(Dr. Ian C Allen, courtesy of The Transport Treasury)

of the Branch.

A steam locomotive returned to the recently closed section at Bartlow in 1969 when the film *Virgin Soldiers* was shot. It featured Stanier Class Black 5 44871, which was disguised as Malaysian locomotive 531.03 and fitted with side tanks, a headlight and a cow catcher. It was craned into a newly dug hole and was surrounded by twisted track.

In 1974 as a result of an energy crisis and the consequent threat of petrol rationing, the Branch was granted an indefinite reprieve in the interests of the local community. The closure order was not implemented and the line remained open.

The line was therefore reduced to what was then called a 'basic railway', being just one line of track without turnouts or any signalling between Marks Tey and Sudbury controlled by a Tyers No.9 token taken by the branch train driver from a room on the Sudbury platform at Marks Tey. In general, the track consisted of standard 95lb bullhead rail of 60ft and 45ft lengths on wooden sleepers, and was last known to have been re-laid in 1956.

In 1982 members of the Stour Valley Railway Preservation Society dismantled the footbridge at Sudbury, and moved it to Chappel for re-erection, where it came into use in 1984.

Plans for electrification of the branch were drawn up in 1984, including the

The driver of a train from Marks Tey removes his tail lamp soon after arrival at Sudbury on May 18th 1977. This view clearly shows the loading dock which became the site of the current station. Apart from the footbridge which is now at Chappel, everything else is part of history. (John D Mann)

building of a north facing chord from the main line at Marks Tey, which would have enabled through trains from Liverpool Street to Sudbury, giving greater utilisation of rolling stock. This would have meant that for electrification clearances, the platform canopy at Chappel and Wakes Colne Station would have been cut back by 3ft, and there would have been a line of electrification masts on the track bed of platform 2 at Chappel, which would have meant the uplifting of the track in that location which had been recovered from King's Cross Goods Depot and laid by the Society members. Fortunately, (for the Society) a cost benefit analysis and shortage of government funding meant this scheme did not go ahead. The cost of construction of the north to west chord of the triangle at Marks Tey, even though the railway already owned the land, was too prohibitive, and was the final nail in the coffin of the scheme.

The branch was operated by various types of two car diesel multiple units, amongst which were Cravens Class 105, Metro Cammell Class 101, and Derby Class 108s. Unusually from 19th January 1987 a Reading based Class 117 unit worked the branch for some days due to a shortage of Norwich based Class 101 units. This gave the train crews some fun, with the destination blinds showing such places as Paddington and Gatwick Airport! During 1991 and 1993 steam trains returned to

Cravens unit operating the 0752 Marks Tey to Sudbury (indicator wrongly set) across Chappel viaduct on 18th July 1970 (G.R. Mortimer)

the Sudbury line when the East Anglian Railway Museum in conjunction with Network SouthEast operated the 'Stour Valley Steamer' using the Museum's restored Class N7 0-6-2 tank locomotive, which successfully made journeys hauling a three car diesel unit from Marks Tey to Great Cornard and return. Sadly, access to Sudbury was not possible due to the cost of manning the crossing at Great Cornard, which was considered to cut too far into the profit margin. Following withdrawal of the original diesel multiple units, the initial replacement was with single car Class 153 units, hired from Anglia Railways. For publicity, the line was marketed from 14th May 1993 as 'The Lovejoy Line', named after a fictional TV character who dealt in antiques in the area. The launch ceremony – performed by actor Dudley Sutton ('Tinker' in the series) – also doubled as the launch of Class 156 services on the branch, with 156405 performing the honours on the 1217 Marks Tey to Sudbury on that day. Class 156 two car units took over the branch services on the following Monday 17th May. In mid-1994 Anglia lost their allocation of Class 156 units, and the branch reverted to operation by single car Class 153s.

In 1995, during the course of the Colchester area re-signalling, a ground frame was installed at Chappel to control a turnout from the branch to the Museum

N7 69621 with the first steam hauled passenger train on the Sudbury branch for many years soon after departing Marks Tey on a dark and windy 22nd December 1991 at 0834 (G R Mortimer)

lines which had been installed on 28th September 1984 by Community Service workers under the guidance of Museum Permanent Way Supervisor Dr Fred Youell. The purpose of this turnout was to facilitate movement in and transport out of Museum vehicles, previously undertaken by the laborious means of a track slew. The turnout had been recovered from Thurrock by Museum volunteers after being rendered redundant by closure of a cement works prior to the Lakeside redevelopment. The Museum Ground Frame is operated by an Annett's Lock, on a staff obtained from a new ground frame known as Marks Tey Ground Frame just the Sudbury side of Marks Tey Station. The ground frame from Baker's Mill crossing was re-furbished and was then installed as the Museum Ground Frame. A derailer was provided on the Museum side of the connection which has not yet been brought into use, although it is connected and tested, leaving sufficient length to stable a disabled Class 153 single unit railcar if needed.

In 1996, following the privatisation of the railways, the branch came under the aegis of the First Great Eastern Train Operating Company, which, due to all their other lines being electrified, meant that they had to hire in diesel units from the Anglia Train Operating Company.

From September 1997 Anglia Railways withdrew the hire deal for a unit to operate the branch as it was undertaking a refurbishment programme on its fleet, and needed the unit back as cover. The only stock available anywhere in the country

On the first day of Bubble car services 55031 shortly after arriving at Sudbury on September 29th 1997. Note the 'viaduct' logo plus the concerned driver looking back to see if anyone will risk the return journey (J D Mann)

was single car 'Heritage' units of Class 121 dating from 1960, made spare by Silverlink and based at Bletchley. On August 9th 1997 55031 (L131) ran from Bletchley to Colchester and on the following day it worked the 0727 Colchester to Marks Tey and then three round trips over the branch as a trial. Colchester depot was reopened as a maintenance facility especially to look after the Class 121s, although for examinations they would still return to Bletchley. Rumours of a new colour scheme were unfounded, although when 55031 (L131) worked the first day of the all-Class 121 service on 29th September 1997 the 'Network SouthEast' branding had been replaced by First Group 'Great Eastern' branding and on the brake van bodyside was a logo depicting an outline of Chappel Viaduct. These units proved not only unreliable but unable to cope with the heavy morning commuter service, when passengers were often left on the stations due to overcrowding. There was considerable vocal opposition to the introduction of the Class 121 units, with the replacement of modern air braked sliding doors units with vacuum braked slam door units being seen as a retrograde step. Reliability was a serious problem, despite the use of two units coupled together in the peaks when availability permitted: regular service suspensions due to no working unit being available led to Great Eastern having to arrange for a bus to be on permanent standby at Marks Tey at a not inconsiderable cost. It was intended that the Class 121s would operate for a maximum of twelve months as agreed with the Franchising Director: it came as a relief to travellers on the line when Anglia Railways were able once again to hire a Class 153 to Great Eastern from 20th July 1998, two months before the deadline for removal of the Class 121. Latterly the Class 121s were operated in pairs all day whenever availability permitted, and on their last day in service - Sunday 19th July 1998 - many enthusiasts were present to record their passing. Colchester depot closed again with their withdrawal. For many years, no service operated on a winter Sunday.

On 18th May 1997 Mount Bures and Cornard level crossings were converted to locally monitored automatic barrier (ABCL) operation. The distant signals on the approach to each crossing, also the Up Home signal at Cornard level crossing, were abolished. Soon afterwards, on 15th September 1997, the start of restoration work on Chappel viaduct by Jackson Contractors was launched with a ceremony re-enacting the laying of the foundation stone in 1847. This was followed on 19th October 1997 by the line being resignalled, with One Train Working where a train staff is not provided introduced. The same weekend, Marks Tey signal box closed and was demolished.

January 1998 brought exceptional flooding to the Stour Valley and the embankment north of Bures was breached, causing a bus service to operate between Bures and Sudbury. The name 'The Lovejoy Line' was forgotten when the television series fell out of favour, and First Great Eastern then marketed the line under the name of 'The Gainsborough Line' from 4th July 1999, after the famous artist of that name well connected with the market town of Sudbury at the terminus of the line.

An increase in passenger numbers on the Marks Tey to Sudbury line during 2000 meant that the accommodation provided on a single Class 153 was no longer adequate at peak times. First Great Eastern hired a road coach to supplement the busiest trains from 25th September 2000, operating non stop between Sudbury and Marks Tey: it left Sudbury for Marks Tey at 0650 with the return journey at 1833. FGE had hoped to hire a two car Class 150 from Anglia Railways, but Anglia required all the sets to maintain its own advertised services.

On 12th January 2001 just before 0900 a track inspector patrolling the branch saw that a landslip affecting the track had occurred. This was near to the junction with the main line at Marks Tey and fortunately the branch unit was at Marks Tey and not trapped by the incident. The line reopened on 22nd January 2001, a bus service running in the interim.

Particularly severe freezing conditions on 1st February 2001 led to an incident at Mount Bures where a car slid off the road on the level crossing and finished up on the track as the 0634 from Sudbury was slowly approaching. The car driver had gone to alert the signaller but this was too late to prevent 153322 from striking the car. The emergency services were called out, as was a coach to take the passengers on to Marks Tey. A police car was the first to arrive and it too skidded on the ice, ending up in a garden. The coach then arrived, ahead of a fire engine which skidded into the coach as it was loading up. The branch was closed for the rest of the day and a bus service put in operation.

On 22nd April 2001 a Class 121 DMU returned to the line, albeit for one round

The crew of 150255 (Driver unknown, Conductor Pete Duly) prepare to depart with the 1629 Marks Tey to Sudbury on 29th April 2005 (J. D. Mann)

trip only and not in public service. It was used in a joint Railtrack / Balfour Beatty scheme to video all lines in Essex. In May 2001 Railtrack announced that some of the residual land they owned at Sudbury would be used for a new bus – rail interchange, with Babergh Council and Roy's Supermarket also providing some land. To date nothing has happened, and the bus and rail stations are an inconvenient five minute walk apart.

Anglia Railways were able to hire a two car Class 150 unit to operate the Sudbury branch with the start of the summer 2001 timetable: for this four new prefabricated platforms were built on top of the platforms at Marks Tey on 21st May 2001 due to the gap between the doors and the platform. Unlike the single car Class 153s (which continued to work at weekends) the Class 150s have their doors more centrally located, which means that the doors do not match up to the curves on the platform. Separate stop boards were provided for Class 150 and Class 153 units at the same time.

In June 2001, on the occasion of a model railway show at the Museum, Platform 2 at Chappel was occupied by the preserved 3 car Class 306 electric unit from Ilford Depot, hauled onto the Museum site by Freightliner Class 66 diesel locomotive number 66 502 which also remained as an added attraction.

In 2001, under new parameters drawn up by Railtrack, and followed by their

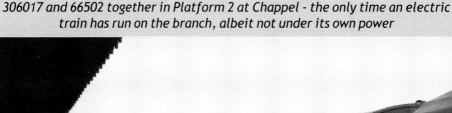

306017 and 66502 together in Platform 2 at Chappel - the only time an electric train has run on the branch, albeit not under its own power

successors Network Rail, the whole of the branch track was due to be re-laid, a section of about 1 mile near Sudbury being so treated with pressed steel sleepers and continuously welded flat bottom rail, and in July 2005, a three mile section from Mount Bures Crossing to Chappel Viaduct was similarly done, but the section through Chappel and Wakes Colne Station used concrete sleepers. To enable the rest of the branch to be done, the line was closed from 10th to 24th July 2005, from 23rd July to 7th August 2006 and from 7th to 15th July 2007.

Following policy from the Strategic Rail Authority, since 2004 the line has come under the initiative of the Essex and South Suffolk Community Rail Partnership, hopefully leading to more local input into management of the line.

The line has also been traversed by steam trains on excursions, including an ex-Southern Railway Merchant Navy Class pacific steam locomotive 'Canadian Pacific' in 2004. Over the years most types of main line diesel locomotives have used the branch on engineering and weedkilling trains, and for delivery of stock to the Museum.

Following a change in the franchise on 1st April 2004, the train operating company 'One' (part of National Express, and renamed National Express East Anglia from 27th February 2008) took over operations, and in 2005 introduced Class 156 two car units during the weekdays, with the service continuing with the Class 153 single car units at weekends. Due to heavy passenger loadings on Saturdays, a pair of Class 153s were diagrammed from September 2007, but this proved short-lived when the franchise had to return three Class 153s to the leasing company in November 2007.

Six people were hurt on 27th January 2006 when a busy passenger train hit the buffers at Sudbury railway station, throwing commuters to the floor. An investigation was immediately launched into the incident, which involved the 6.05 pm train from Marks Tey to Sudbury formed by 156422. An East Anglian Ambulance Service spokeswoman said that nobody was seriously hurt, and those injured were treated at the scene. After official investigations on site had concluded, the unit was towed away the next day by 153335. The subsequent inquiry concluded that the cause of the accident was driver error.

The Line Today

Even in its reduced form, the Stour Valley line retains much of its charm and attraction. The branch diverges from the main line at the Colchester end of Marks Tey station, and is served by a single curving platform behind the down mainline platform. The line then curves away towards the north-west on an embankment, crosses the little Roman River and, rising at 1 in 147, enters a long cutting. After climbing for about a mile, the line becomes level for a short distance, and then descends at 1 in 159 into the Colne Valley, curving to the north-east. The River Colne and the main Halstead road are then crossed by the Chappel Viaduct, from which a fine view of the valley is obtained. There is an upward gradient of about 1 in 120, to cater for which each arch of the viaduct is three inches higher than the next one going northwards. Chappel & Wakes Colne Station adjoins the northern end of the viaduct and its two platforms may be seen, although only the former down platform is in use by both British Rail and the East Anglian Railway Museum. Unfortunately should plans to electrify the Sudbury Branch ever come to fruition it would necessitate certain alterations and amongst these is the cutting back of three feet of the delightful awning. The loss of this would be a great pity as the architectural styling of Chappel is very unusual amongst GER rural stations, and its canopy adds a great deal of character. The exterior of Chappel Station is little altered from GE days except the stairway from ground level which is now exposed to the elements, and not covered as before. The buildings on Platform 2 were demolished in the late 1960s by British Rail when the line became a 'basic railway', although some traces of the footings remain. Nevertheless the structure possesses much charm, and is worthy of inspection.

Passing the restored signal box, built in 1891 by the Great Eastern Railway on land owned by the Colne Valley Railway, the line passes under Spring Gardens Road bridge, 50 yards north of which the track bed of the Colne Valley line curved off to the left, and the Stour Valley line then climbs an incline ascending at 1 in 121-103 which carries it in a deep cutting up to the ridge which separates the valleys of

'One' Railway liveried 156407 (advertising the Wherry Lines) slows for the Chappel stop on 6th September 2007

the Colne and the Stour. From the summit of the ridge, a magnificent panorama is presented of the Stour Valley countryside, with its rich farm lands. The line descends steeply for two miles at 1 in 90, past Mount Bures level crossing, and reaches the Stour Valley at Bures. In the early 1970s the station building still possessed the old belfry which once housed the train arrival bell, rung in the early days for each train. The station canopy was removed from the single platform in the early 1970s thus restoring it to its original condition as built in 1849, but the building has now been demolished and replaced by a meagre shelter.

The Stour Valley here continues northwards, and the line follows its course for the rest of the journey to Sudbury. (The line beyond Sudbury continued to follow the river as far as Stoke.) The main Colchester to Sudbury road also runs parallel to the railway. Between Bures and Sudbury the line crosses the river into Suffolk and runs along the water meadows past Cornard level crossing, where the former siding has been removed, and then curves to the west to enter Sudbury station, passing on the down side the site of the signal box which latterly controlled only two signals – the down home and the up starter, controlling the entrance to and the exit from the only remaining platform line. Gradients on the section from Bures are negligible. The former goods yard at Sudbury is now bereft of its tracks and the original

A bridge between Sudbury and Long Melford in December 2005 (Mark House)

station building at the north end has been demolished. The main booking office and station was used for a time as a museum of local history, and the booking hall and office rented by the SVRPS as a base should running on the branch become possible, but continued vandalism put an end to this idea, and the local history museum was closed following a fire. In 1985/6 the former goods yard at Sudbury, previously the site of the original station, was demolished. The site is now occupied by a supermarket building, originally a Solar superstore but now trading as Roy's supermarket.

After a period of being boarded up and neglected, the station buildings were demolished to make way for a new swimming pool and leisure centre with car park. Despite the dereliction, the platform continued to be used for trains, until the new development caused a new platform to be built on the bed of the previous vehicle loading dock, with a bus type shelter: this opened on 28th October 1990.

Beyond the site of Sudbury station, the track bed continues close to the river, and is now in use as a public footpath, continuing towards Long Melford, where the station buildings have now become a private residence, and the maltings which the goods yard served have also been similarly converted. The trackbed has been infilled to platform level and grassed over. New housing has been built at both ends of the station. For many years part of the station yard

Glemsford station on 23rd September 2007: note the very dilapidated level crossing gate still just about surviving

was in use by Theobalds Coaches, whose name lives on with Theobalds Close forming part of the housing development here. At the next station, Glemsford, the old station house has been much altered and made into a private residence, as has the goods shed, which still retains its nice wooden canopy. The platforms and station buildings have, however, all been demolished.

The old crossing keeper's house at Cavendish survives as a dwelling, but only a fragment of platform continues to adjoin it. The station buildings here were demolished even before the track was lifted and new housing was built: the rest disappeared in the 1970s.

The same cannot be said of the next station, Clare, which has been incorporated into a country park, and has been pleasantly restored. Both platforms are complete with their attendant buildings, and the goods shed has been provided with a short section of track provided by the East Anglian Railway Museum and installed under its supervision. For some years a former British Rail box van was stored on this track, housing a collection of local railway photographs: many of these are now on display in the goods shed, which has been turned into a visitors centre.

Stoke is also largely intact and a private house, although the trackbed has been filled to platform level, and the canopy has been removed. Originally the line crossed the village green, but all trace of this is now gone and the

Clare station on 16th May 2004

50

Long Melford station on 12th June 1993

green is restored.

Sturmer station is now tucked away behind trees and bushes and appears to be very secluded. The main building has been rendered over and is a private house, and the platform incorporated into the garden.

Haverhill lost its buildings around 1970, although the site has remained derelict. The site was purchased by Tesco in 2003 as the location for a new store but no work has taken place so far. At Bartlow the Stour Valley line platforms have been infilled, but all the station buildings remain intact as a private residence called 'The Booking Hall'.

Linton has all buildings and part of the platforms remaining: the station house is in use as a school, whilst the station building is an office. The station, station house, yard and public house at Pampisford were all obliterated in the interests of dualling the A11. Shelford survives as a working station (albeit unstaffed) serving the Liverpool Street to Cambridge trains; part of the up side buildings now houses an Indian restaurant.

On the branch from Long Melford to Bury, Welnetham has been adapted for private use but the main structure has survived. At Cockfield the single storey building at Cockfield is still standing, albeit tatty, but the splendid cast iron urinal has been removed, and now restored to working order at Chappel. An unusual Royal Mail post box is located in the overbridge here, and is still in use. At Lavenham, all traces of the station have disappeared under an industrial estate.

51

Train Services Today

As on many other rural branches, passenger traffic is easily observed as divided into two types, peak and off peak. The Monday to Friday timings include a first departure from Sudbury at 0530, and the last at 2200. Both make connections at Marks Tey but carry passengers no further. For many years, before the main line trains were both accelerated and increased in frequency, the branch trains ran through to Colchester St. Botolphs, now known as Colchester Town. This was really useful for Sudbury residents – especially for shoppers - but was cut back to the bay platform at Colchester North and eventually withdrawn to run only from the Sudbury platform at Marks Tey, becoming just a shuttle running between Marks Tey and Sudbury. This initially had a very negative effect on the number of off-peak travellers. However, by keeping the train as a branch shuttle it enabled an hourly service to be operated off peak instead of the previous service of one every two hours. The only bright spot in the daily timetable is the service at 1640 from Sudbury which is non-stop to Marks Tey. Its passage down the hill from Bures non-stop through Chappel is 'interesting' to the unsuspecting observer sitting on Platform 1. The matching 0740 non-stop from Marks Tey to Sudbury is not so much interesting as irritating, with intending Sudbury passengers having to wait another 35 minutes for the next train!

Facts & Figures

Stour Valley Line Headcodes

Many different headcodes have been in use on the Stour Valley line, the earliest of which I have details being those employed after the Eastern Counties Railway assumed the working of the line on 1st January, 1854.

In the case of all ordinary trains, the locomotive was required to carry one white light on top of the smoke box, together with a red light, presumably on the buffer beam. This was the standard headcode for all ECR single lines, and the sensible practice of requiring trains on single lines to carry a red light in front is believed to have been unique, first to the ECR, and then to its successor the GER, which continued it. In addition to the lamps mentioned above, special trains also had to carry a white board by day and a second white lamp by night.

With the growth of its system in the seventies and eighties of the last century the GER gradually evolved its complex code of locomotive headlights. The standard single line headcode, which applied to the Stour Valley line during the early days of the GER required a red light on the smoke box and a white light on the buffer beam in the case of all ordinary trains. Special trains had an additional white light by night or a white disc by day, on the buffer beam.

By this time, on other parts of the system, the GER had introduced coloured discs for daytime use, and these always consisted of the basic colour in the centre, with a white rim.

By 1891, the Marks Tey, Sudbury and Bury line had headcodes peculiar to itself. By day, ordinary trains merely carried a green disc at the right-hand end of the buffer beam, while special trains had an additional white disc on the smoke box. By night, ordinary trains carried a green light at the right-hand end of the buffer beam, and a red light on the smoke box. Special trains by night carried a red light on the smoke box and, on the buffer beam, a green light at the right-hand end and a white light at the left hand end.

On the Sudbury-Cambridge section, the ordinary single-line headcode was employed between Sudbury and Shelford, this consisting, in the case of ordinary trains, of a red disc on the smoke box by day, and, by night, of a red light on the smoke box and a white light on the left-hand end of the buffer beam. Special trains by day bore a red disc on the smoke box and a white disc in the centre of the buffer beam, while by night they carried a red light on the smoke box with two white lights, one at each end of the buffer beam.

4.38pm Marks Tey to Haverhill starting out, hauled by J15 65432 with side window cab and tender cab for working the Colne Valley line.
5th October 1957. (G. R. Mortimer)

In 1903, the standard single line headcodes, applicable still between Sudbury and Shelford, were changed. Ordinary trains by day continued to carry just a red disc on the smoke box, but by night they bore a red light on the smoke box and a green light on the left-hand end of the buffer beam. Special trains carried, by day, a red disc on the smoke box and a white disc on the left-hand end of the buffer beam, and by night, a red light on the smoke box, a green light on the left-hand end of the buffer beam and a white light on the right-hand end. The headcodes for the Marks Tey, Sudbury and Bury line remained unaltered.

By 1910, the distinction between ordinary and special trains was abolished, as was the difference in headcodes for day and night working, save only, of course, that discs were used by day and lamps by night. The headcode for the Marks Tey, Sudbury and Bury line now consisted of a red disc or lamp on the smoke box and green disc or lamp on the right-hand end of the buffer beam, while the standard single line code, used between Sudbury and Shelford, comprised a red disc or lamp on the smoke-box and a green disc or lamp on the left-hand end of the buffer beam.

After the Grouping, the London and North Eastern Railway Company decided that the use of green lights and discs in headcodes constituted a possible source

J20 64678 on a freight shunting at Cockfield
(Dr I C Allen, courtesy of The Transport Treasury)

of danger, and from 1926 onwards superseded them with violet lights and discs as the latter became available. In 1927, the LNER simplified the system of headcodes in use on the former GER lines, abolishing the special headcodes applicable to single lines generally and to a number of country branches in particular, including the Marks Tey, Sudbury and Bury line. From that date, all trains on the Stour Valley lines carried the headcodes standard throughout the British Railways generally (except the Southern Railway), so as to indicate the class and description of the train concerned. Ex-GER locomotives and locomotives built to work upon the GE section continued to use white discs by day and lamps by night, but as other locomotives migrated to the GE section, lamps were to be seen also by day, until in later British Railways days, the former GE discs became comparatively rare before the final abolition of steam traction. Some diesel locomotives were fitted with discs, but these disappeared with the number indications which replaced the old system of headcodes.

Some Examples of Fares and Fastest Timings Between London and Sudbury

		Single Fares			Fastest Timings (minutes)	
Date	1st cl.	2nd cl.	3rd cl.	Parly	Down	Up
September 1849	13/-	9/9	6/9	4/10	148	175
January 1856	14/-	10/9	8/-	4/10	135	135
August 1865 Exp.	13/6	9/6	7/3	4/10	115	120
August 1865 Ord.	12/-					
November 1875	11/-	8/6	6/6	4/10	110	128
October 1883	11/-1	8/6	4/11½	-	105	117
May 1894	11/-	-	4/11½	-	97	117
October 1905	11/-	-	4/11½	-	102	115
October 1914	11/-	-	4/11½	-	91	87
October 1922	12/4	-	7/5	-	103	98
October 1930	12/5	-	7/6	-	102	99
October 1938	13/-	-	7/11	-	99	96
October 1947	20/2	-	12/3	-	111	115
October 1956	13/11	9/3	-	-	93	95
July 1965	24/-	16/-	-	-	83	85
September 1969	-	15/-*	-	-	80	83
June 1972	-	£1.15*	-	-	80	84
October 1987	-	£8.00	-	-	76	81
January 2006	£30.40	£19.50	-	-	69	69

- No through bookings: the sum quoted is the sum of the fares from Liverpool Street to Marks Tey and from Marks Tey to Sudbury.

Notes:
1. First class "express" fares were introduced on 1st January, 1857 and discontinued on 1st September, 1870.
2. Parliamentary fares were abolished, and third class ordinary fares reduced to approximately the former parliamentary level, on 1st October, 1883.
3. Second class on the GER outside the London suburban area was abolished on 1st May, 1893, except on the Continental boat trains.

Stour Valley Permanent Speed Restrictions

The first mention of a speed restriction on the Stour Valley line which I have been able to trace is to be found in the Great Eastern Railway Working Time Table for October 1866, which provides that "No Engine or Train, Up or Down, is to pass over any portion of the line between Marks Tey and Sudbury at a greater speed than 20 Miles an Hour."

In April 1868, the following restrictions are shown:-
Marks Tey Station: All Up Sudbury Branch Trains and Light engines are to come to a stand on the Branch clear of the Main Line.
Chappel Station: All Up and Down Trains and Light Engines are to stop.
Melford Station: All Trains and Light Engines coming off the Cambridge Line are to come to a stand at the Junction, clear of the Sudbury and Bury Main Line.
Welnetham Station: No Down Train or Engine is to pass through at a greater speed than 10 miles an hour.

By October 1870, the restriction at Welnetham had been eased to 15 m.p.h.; by February 1875, an additional restriction had appeared at Chappel, where a speed limit of 5 m.p.h. for both up and down trains and engines applied over the points at the Marks Tey end of the station.

The GER Appendix to the Working Time Tables for January 1891 shows a restriction to 15 m.p.h. in each direction over the curve between Sudbury and Long Melford, as well as the requirement for trains from the Cambridge line to come to a stand at Long Melford Junction. By 1893, the latter requirement had disappeared, but there was an additional restriction to 10 m.p.h. for up trains through Sturmer station.

There had been, at least since 1891, a general restriction of speed to 10 m.p.h. for running through any hand-worked points, and in 1908, a similar speed restriction was imposed for all trains when exchanging staffs and tablets by hand on single lines.

In 1919, a further speed restriction to 45 m.p.h. was imposed for all trains when passing over the curve between Withersfield Siding and Bartlow, and in 1927 a speed restriction to 20 m.p.h. was introduced through Sudbury station. Also introduced at that time was a general restriction to 20 m.p.h. for all trains running through loop connections on single lines.

By 1937, a speed restriction to 15 m.p.h. had been introduced for Stour Valley line trains passing over the junction with the Cambridge main line at Shelford, but the speed limit over the curve between Sudbury and Long Melford had been relaxed to 20 m.p.h., while the speed restriction at Sturmer had been withdrawn entirely. In August 1938, a restriction to 40 m.p.h. was imposed over the whole section between Bartlow and Shelford, and later in the same year restrictions to 50 m.p.h. were introduced over the entire sections between Long Melford and Bury St. Edmunds. In 1939, an additional 10 m.p.h. restriction was imposed over Underline Bridge No. 910, between Sudbury and Long Melford, and on the outbreak of war the general restriction to 60 m.p.h. was applied to all lines not having a lower restriction.

The LNER Appendix to the Working Time Tables, operative from 4th May 1942, introduced a 50 m.p.h. speed restriction between Marks Tey and Chappel, reintroduced the 10 m.p.h. limit over the underline bridge referred to above, reduced the limit between Withersfield and Bartlow to 40 m.p.h., and imposed a restriction at Bury Junction for trains to and from Long Melford to 20 m.p.h., besides retaining all the previously existing restrictions.

The last LNER Appendix, dated 1st November 1947, repeated all the above restrictions except that over the underline bridge, which was again abolished, and by 1956 the general 50 m.p.h. limit applied to the whole of the line between Marks Tey and Bartlow, while the limit between Long Melford and Bury St. Edmunds was reduced to 40 m.p.h.

In 1964, an additional restriction to 25 m.p.h. had been imposed over the curve approaching Shelford from the Stour Valley line, and the general restriction over the truncated line from Bury St. Edmunds to Lavenham, now open to freight only, had been reduced to 25 m.p.h. between Bury St. Edmunds and Welnetham and 20 m.p.h. between Welnetham and Lavenham.

On the remaining portion of the Stour Valley line now in operation, the general restriction to 50 m.p.h. still subsists, with a restriction to 20 m.p.h. through the junction at Marks Tey, and a 5 m.p.h. restriction in and out of the platform at Marks Tey.

A brief history of developments at Chappel & Wakes Colne

The Stour Valley Railway Preservation Society was formed on September 24th 1968, with the object of preserving all or part of the recently closed Sudbury to Shelford line. The stretch of line finally selected as being most suitable for this purpose was that from Sudbury to Long Melford, a distance of some three miles. Due to lack of funding this rather ambitious project was unsuccessful, and the line was lost.

This failure necessitated a complete reappraisal of the Society's structure, and in 1970 the Branch Line Preservation Company Ltd. was formed. Company status was required in order to formally negotiate with British Rail the take over of a branch line which was still open but destined for closure. Obviously the primary objective was the Marks Tey – Sudbury branch, leaving open the option of considering alternative endangered lines.

The headquarters of the SVRPS was established at Chappel and Wakes Colne Station in December 1969. A lease was obtained from British Rail on the redundant goods yard, goods shed, signal box and station buildings.

The members were faced with a daunting task. The site was derelict and without electricity, and the track had been dismantled in preparation for removal.

An early steam day at Chappel with 'Gunby' (Fred Tanton)

Despite all this, the first public steaming took place less than a hundred days later. The only operational loco 0-6-0ST 'Gunby' carried passengers in a contractor's weighing van over a third of a mile of re-laid track. In the following months a miscellany of rolling stock and locos arrived, the most important being class S.15 loco No. 30841. The restoration of this fine machine was assisted by funding from a long-established Suffolk brewing company, and in commemoration of this it received the name 'Greene King' during a ceremony on the platform at Bury St Edmunds on July 7th 1975.

A further significant achievement occurred in 1973 when the SVRPS became the first preservation society to slew a BR running line to allow stock to enter the site. Shortly after, a second slew facilitated the arrival of the GER designed N.7 loco No. 69621. However, most rolling stock arrived by road, the largest item being the ex-BR Class 4 2-6-4T No. 80151 in 1975, and previously mentioned S15.

The buildings were quickly restored; the goods shed being used as a workshop and part of the station buildings being taken over as a book and gift shop, then and now a major source of funding.

In the late 1970s with the continued presence of BR on the branch much frustration and dissent was evident within the Society. The loss of a few prominent locomotives, notably 'Greene King', to other locations, only made the situation worse. Dwindling attendances and lack of membership participation led to a period of stagnation.

In the early 1980s it was realised there was a need for a change in the function of the Chappel site, which would need to become more of a public attraction with improved facilities. The advent of a footbridge enabled unsupervised crossing of the BR line by visitors on steam days, removing the obligation and expense of employing a BR crossing keeper.

An attempt at this stage to run steam on the Branch on Sundays awakened a resurgence of interest in the Society and its activities. The albeit less ambitious plan to run steam between Chappel and Marks Tey was rejected by BR due to a lack of suitable locomotives, amongst other reasons. However a consequence of this was the relaying of track along platform 2 and the construction of a permanent turnout linking the site with BR track.

In 1983 the company purchased, on behalf of the Society, a plot of land, and constructed an engine restoration shed and workshop. The shed had originally been used during the building of the Dartford Tunnel, and had been purchased by the Society some years previously. This project involved a great deal of moving and track laying and showed to the full the dedication and commitment of the membership. 1985 saw the rescue and re-erection of the signal box from Mistley

'Jubilee' on a demonstration train at Chappel on 6th May 2007

Class 04 diesel locomotive passing the ex-Mistley signal box on 26th June 1999 (G D King)

Station, a Grade 1 listed building, purchased for the princely sum of £5! This box has been fully restored and now controls most of the signalling and points on the site. The Goods Shed was also restored to its former glory at this time, and is now used for exhibitions and functions.

In addition to enormous contributions from the membership, much of the work on site has been achieved with the assistance of Community Service programmes, Manpower Services Commission Community Programmes, Youth Training Scheme projects and other organisations such as the Eastern Electricity Board Young Persons Development Project.

The present policy of the Museum includes the running of the Chappel site as a museum, a living archive for the benefit and enjoyment of the community.

Whilst the Society had for some years been attempting to negotiate purchase of the site from the British Railway Property Board, the Board's insistence on a totally unrealistic price well beyond its market value and out of reach of the Society's finances doomed this to failure, but in 1987 the Board forced the issue and put the site on the market by auction, in which the Society's legal entity Branch Line Preservation Company Limited were the successful bidders, with financial help by way of sale of the Society's locomotive number 80151 to a group of members.

With the future of the site assured, fundraising continued by operating Steam Days under the titles of Chappel Steam Centre, and the Stour Valley Railway, but many visitors complained, expecting a ride on the branch rather than just the length of the goods yard. A reappraisal of operations was therefore undertaken, and with the realisation that the Society had gathered together a wide collection of all types of rolling stock and railway equipment from, in the main, East Anglia, the decision was taken to change the name of the organisation to the East Anglian Railway Museum, which went ahead in 1986.

The transfer of ownership of the site had led to the requirement to obtain a Light Railway Order to regularise the running of trains, and this was granted in 1991, being known as The Chappel and Wakes Colne Light Railway, with operation vested in the East Anglian Railway Museum, which by then had become a company limited by guarantee, with charitable status also being granted in 1991. EARM became a Registered Museum in 1999, and in the same year the 150th Anniversary of the opening of the Colchester, Sudbury, Stour Valley and Halstead Railway was celebrated in grand style at Chappel in conjunction with the launch of the Gainsborough Line name, the Museum supplying a re-enactment of the opening train complete with guests in period clothes and a brass band. A splendid occasion!

For nearly forty years now the Museum and its predecessors have struggled to conserve a historically significant representation of our regional railway heritage, and largely through the efforts of its volunteers, thousands of visitors annually enjoy the working of the Museum that is the Chappel experience, and the intention is that it will continue to develop and bring a slice of living history into the lives of future generations.

The future undoubtedly holds many further challenges. The possible electrification of the Branch would bring problems which will have to be overcome. This may necessitate the purchase of adjacent land upon which to run the Museum's own stock if access to BR track is rendered impossible.

The museum has worked tirelessly to conserve a historically significant representation of our regional railway heritage over many years. Largely through the efforts of its volunteers, thousands of visitors annually enjoy the working museum that is the Chappel Experience.

The intention is that it will continue to bring a working reminder of East Anglian railway heritage into the lives of generations to come, and continue to preserve the past for the future.

Captions for back cover photographs: the top photograph by J. D. Mann shows a glorious day in the Stour Valley on May 16th 1998, when 55029 climbs away from Mount Bures towards Chappel with an afternoon service from Sudbury. The lower photograph by G. R. Mortimer shows a Gloucester Carriage & Wagon Company DMU crossing Pitmire Bridge over the River Stour on 29th September 1973.

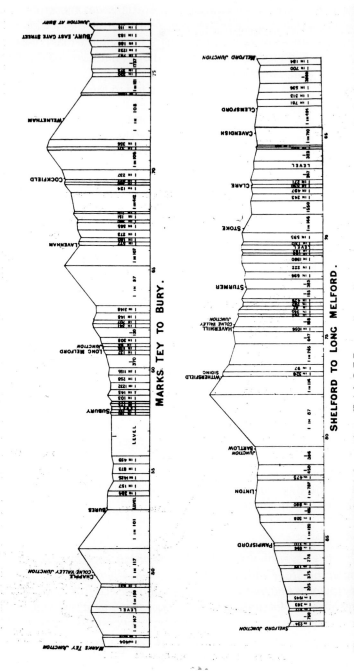

MARKS TEY TO BURY.

SHELFORD TO LONG MELFORD.

These diagrams are reproduced from the official G.E.R. gradient diagrams drawn in 1894. The gradients shown will be found to differ slightly from those mentioned in the text of this book, which are taken from the British Railways signal box diagrams produced in about 1950

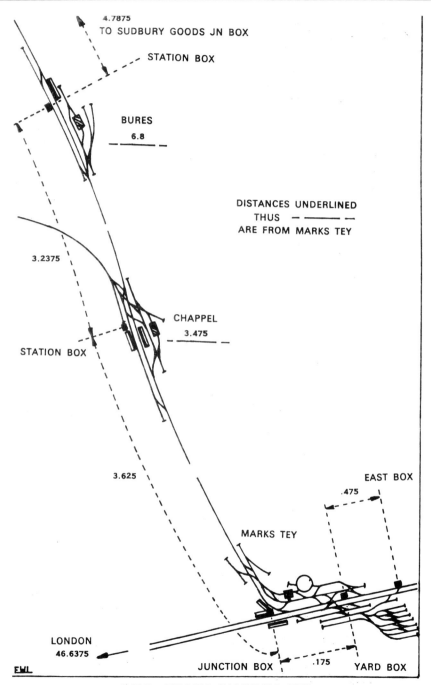

4.7875
TO SUDBURY GOODS JN BOX

STATION BOX

BURES
6.8

DISTANCES UNDERLINED
THUS — —————— —
ARE FROM MARKS TEY

3.2375

CHAPPEL
3.475

STATION BOX

3.625

EAST BOX
.475

MARKS TEY

LONDON
46.6375

FWL

JUNCTION BOX
.175

YARD BOX

G.E.R. TRACK DIAGRAM 1918

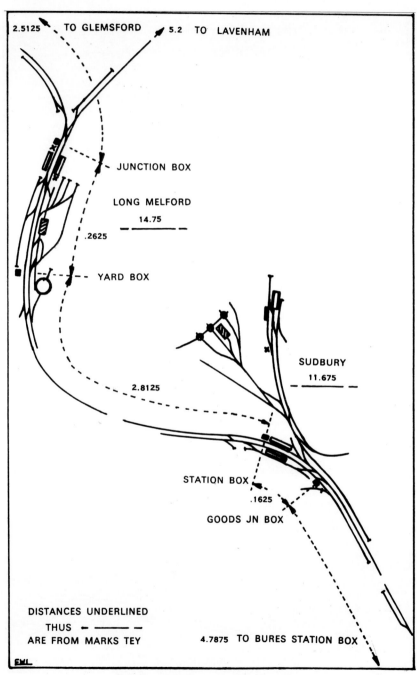

2.5125　TO GLEMSFORD　5.2　TO LAVENHAM

JUNCTION BOX

LONG MELFORD
14.75 —

.2625

YARD BOX

SUDBURY
11.675 —

2.8125

STATION BOX

.1625

GOODS JN BOX

DISTANCES UNDERLINED
THUS — ——— —
ARE FROM MARKS TEY

4.7875　TO BURES STATION BOX

G.E.R. TRACK DIAGRAM 1918

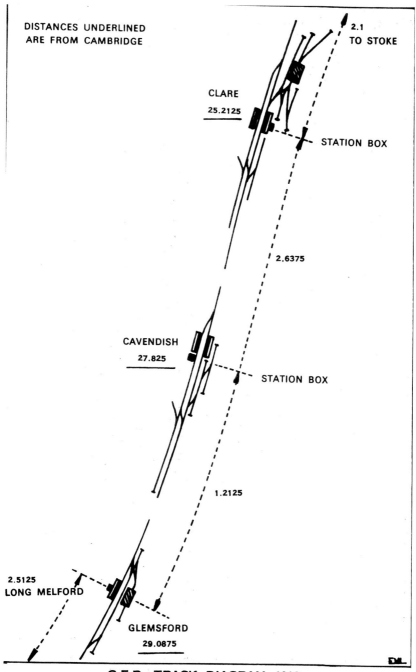

DISTANCES UNDERLINED
ARE FROM CAMBRIDGE

2.1
TO STOKE

CLARE
25.2125

STATION BOX

2.6375

CAVENDISH
27.825

STATION BOX

1.2125

2.5125
LONG MELFORD

GLEMSFORD
29.0875

G.E.R. TRACK DIAGRAM 1918

65

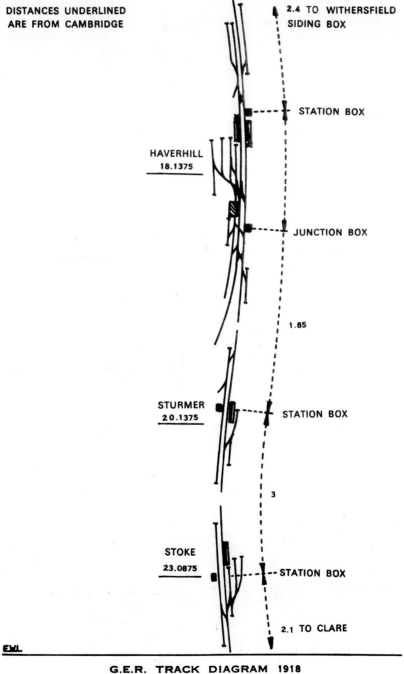

DISTANCES UNDERLINED ARE FROM CAMBRIDGE

2.4 TO WITHERSFIELD SIDING BOX

STATION BOX

HAVERHILL
18.1375

JUNCTION BOX

1.85

STURMER
20.1375

STATION BOX

3

STOKE
23.0875

STATION BOX

2.1 TO CLARE

EWL

G.E.R. TRACK DIAGRAM 1918

66

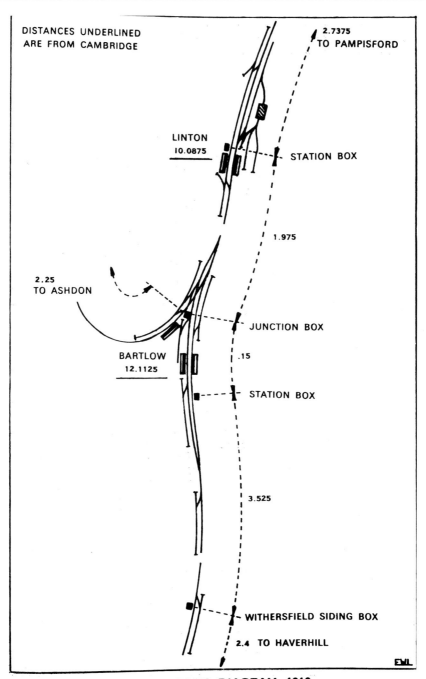

DISTANCES UNDERLINED
ARE FROM CAMBRIDGE

2.7375
TO PAMPISFORD

LINTON
10.0875

STATION BOX

1.975

2.25
TO ASHDON

JUNCTION BOX

BARTLOW
12.1125

.15

STATION BOX

3.525

WITHERSFIELD SIDING BOX

2.4 TO HAVERHILL

EWL

G.E.R. TRACK DIAGRAM 1918

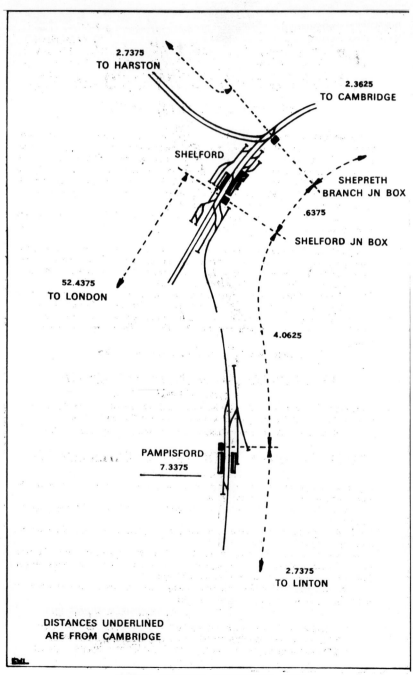

2.7375
TO HARSTON

2.3625
TO CAMBRIDGE

SHELFORD

SHEPRETH
BRANCH JN BOX

.6375

SHELFORD JN BOX

52.4375
TO LONDON

4.0625

PAMPISFORD
7.3375

2.7375
TO LINTON

DISTANCES UNDERLINED
ARE FROM CAMBRIDGE

G.E.R. TRACK DIAGRAM 1918